TIME'S
WINGED CHARIOT

The Story of a Humberside Childhood
at the Turn of the Century

by
T. BERNARD HEALD

"But at my back I always hear
Time's wingéd chariot hurrying near. . ."
From Andrew Marvell: "To his coy mistress"

HUTTON PRESS
1985

Hutton Press Ltd.
130 Canada Drive, Cherry Burton, Beverley
North Humberside, HU17 7SB

*Printed by Clifford Ward & Co.
(Bridlington) Ltd.*

Cover: Holderness Road, Hull, c.1900

ISBN 0 907033 26 1

To my Parents
Tom and Susan Heald

FOREWORD

This book covers a personal history and recollections of the region now known as Humberside during the first two decades of the present century, as seen through the eyes of a boy who attained the age of fifteen years shortly after the end of the First World War.

Why did I write it? It seemed to me, looking back, that this period was a momentous one in our nation's history, and particularly so for Humberside. My memories of events in those days are remarkably vivid, and the contrast between life in Edwardian days and today seemed to call for pen to paper. Encouraged by my wife, who also had in mind the importance of letting grandchildren know something of the humour, trauma and disciplines of those times, the idea of a written account gradually evolved.

The story starts in Hull where I was born, moves into North Lincolnshire with life by the edge of the great Humber estuary, and returns to Hull again. It covers schooldays, family tragedy, the First World War with the "Zep" raids on Hull, and my reluctant introduction to commercial life at the age of thirteen. Yet through it all there runs the thread of adventure and fun, without which human life would be the poorer.

T.B.H.
April 1985

ACKNOWLEDGEMENTS

The author wishes to express his thanks to the Editors of the Daily Mirror, the Yorkshire Post, the Hull and Yorkshire Times and the Yorkshire Ridings Magazine for permission to use extracts originally appearing in their publications; also to Malcolm MacGregor of the Lincolnshire and Humberside Arts Association for his help and encouragement; and to Graham Henderson of the BBC for arranging the script's adaptation and broadcasting on BBC Radio Humberside.

The publishers wish to thank the Ordnance Survey for permission to reproduce part of the 1905 Ordnance Survey map; and Humberside Leisure Services, in particular Chris Barnett, for providing the illustration on the front cover and for their assistance in producing a copy of the 1905 map.

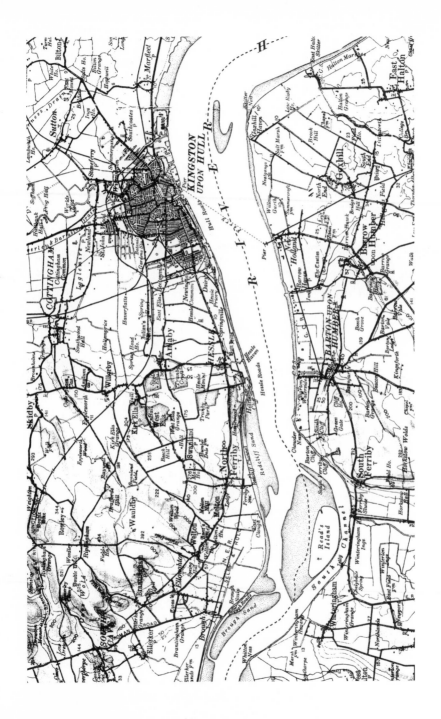

CHAPTER ONE

I was born at No. 68, Fountain Road, Hull, on 20th December 1903. This house no longer exists, for it disappeared under the site clearers' bulldozer in 1976, along with many more in that area. My father was John Thomas Heald, a master shipwright and boatbuilder, and my mother was Susan, only daughter of Samuel and Martha Hollingworth.

At that time, Hull was rapidly developing as a port and industrial centre, providing employment for people drawn in from a wide area. "Opportunity" was the key word which brought each side of my family to Hull in the first place, for they were both incomers from North Lincolnshire. My mother's people had long connections with the agricultural area around Grainthorpe and North Somercotes between Grimsby and Mablethorpe.

My maternal grandmother was born a "Cook," a member of a family well scattered in North and East Yorkshire and Lincolnshire. Probably the most illustrious bearer of the name was Captain James Cook, the explorer, born at Marton-in-Cleveland in 1728, and whose statue gazes out to sea from the West Cliff at Whitby. As it happens, there was a strong link with Cleveland and North Yorkshire on my father's maternal side.

The Healds have had a long and, at times, turbulent history. The first recorded appearance of the family was in the year 1207, when Adam de Helde had lands in North Devon. According to Burke's Landed Gentry, the name means in Old English "residence or dwelling place near a slope." One can imagine them enjoying life in a Devon combe, possibly having been given lands by William the Conqueror, but whether they came over with William in 1066 can only be conjecture. It is more than possible that they were established in the West Country in Anglo-Saxon times in spite of the Normanised version of the name.

Disputes appear to have developed within the family in late medieval or Elizabethan times, and one branch moved north, settling in Lancashire where they were prominent in the development of the cotton industry. The invention of the "heddle" or "heald," a series of vertical cords or wires with a loop or heddle-eye to receive a warp thread, and passing round and between parallel bars, was one of their contributions to the Lancashire cotton industry.

Some of the family moved east, and we hear of them at Bevercotes and Kneesall in Nottinghamshire, from where my great-grandfather moved to North Lincolnshire in 1835. He took over the flour mill at Scawby Brook near Brigg, and this is where my grandfather, George Heald, appears on the scene. He met, fell in love with, and married Alice Dawson of South Ferriby, eldest daughter of William and Mary Dawson, in 1866.

Now, the Dawsons had, some thirty years earlier, moved from the Great Ayton/Stokesley area of North Yorkshire, not half a dozen miles from

Marton, where Captain Cook was born. Was there any significance, I wonder, looking at the maternal wings, in the eventual union of Cook and Dawson progency in the shape of my parents in 1895?

To go back to the Healds. For some years after their marriage George and Alice lived happily enough, and four children were born, all boys, of whom my father, Tom, was the youngest. Then George, as the saying goes, "got into bad company," took to drink, and eventually deserted his wife and family. Naturally, this shocked and upset the Dawsons, who were good Wesleyan Methodists, and by then well-established as farmers and butchers at South Ferriby. However, they stood by Alice and her four boys, whose later childhood days at the village were not unhappy ones.

As they neared school leaving age, it was obvious that opportunities for advancement, apart from farming, were not good, and Alice and family moved to Hull, where Tom was apprenticed as a shipwright at John Brown's yard. This was in 1885, Tom then being fourteen years old. After his apprenticeship was completed he transferred to Earles, the big shipbuilding yard on Hedon Road. Earles were then building a cruiser for the Royal Navy, the *Endymion*, and Tom, who was engaged in its construction, made a wall model of the ship, which I still possess.

During this period he had joined up with the Methodists at Scott Street Chapel, and was soon roped in for its activities, being minute secretary for the Biblical Association in 1890. According to their syllabus, he gave a talk on "Love towards Man" on December 28th of that year. It was at Scott Street Chapel that he met Susan Hollingworth, a teacher at St. Luke's School, whose father Samuel had married Martha Cook in 1869, and was then a journeyman joiner. They were married on 17th October, 1895, Tom's twenty-fourth birthday, Susan being twenty-one.

Their first child, Dorothy, was born on 30th June, 1897. She was a rather delicate child and, according to my parents, "took some rearing." A son, Wilfred Dawson, was born in 1902, but he neither suffered the sorrows nor enjoyed the pleasures of this world, for he only lived three months, and died in an epidemic of infantile dysentery while in hospital for a slight operation, a great sadness to his parents.

When I arrived on 20th December, 1903, hopes were high that I should prove a healthy child. Whether it was due to the fact that I was born on a Sunday, and the old rhyme says "The child that is born on the Sabbath Day is blythe and bonny, and good and gay," the fact was that I seemed to be disgustingly healthy, and suffered few childish ailments apart from measles. Christened Thomas Bernard, I was known to the family as Bernie, and this diminutive remained with me for many years, and within the inner family limits is still sometimes used.

During his latter years at Earles yard, my father had a fall from the rigging of a ship, and suffered internal injuries which, although apparently cleared, were to cause serious trouble later on. Soon after I was born we moved from Fountain Road to No. 49 Sculcoates Lane — "Ferriby House" as we named it. Fountain Road was, in the rapidly growing city, now in the inner belt, and Sculcoates Lane, farther out along the main Beverley road, was a much nicer locality.

About this time, my father went into partnership with two colleagues, and the firm of "Guy, Heald, and Hearson" was born. Guy was the financial backer, and Heald and Hearson provided the technical skill of this firm of ship repairers and boat builders. They had premises and a "hard" in what was known as the Old Harbour at Wilmington, some distance up from the confluence of the River Hull with the Humber.

My recollections of this part of my life up to three years of age are quite vivid. At eighteen months or so, I can remember my mother holding me up to the telephone we had had installed, to speak to "Da-da" and wondering how on earth his answering voice got into the instrument. I can also remember at this time being taken in a push-chair by my sister Dorothy and our cousin Arthur Heald for walks along Beverley Road and into Pearson Park to feed the ducks.

My grandparents on my mother's side, the Hollingworths, lived then near Cannon Street Station, the terminus of the old Hull and Barnsley Railway. The next station on the passenger line was the suburban one of Beverley Road, only a stone's throw from where we lived in Sculcoates Lane. The fare was one penny between the two stations, and it was a favourite outing of ours to have tea with Grandpa and Grandma on Saturdays, returning home in the gas-lit train in the late evening.

Now and again we had a brief visit to see Grandma Heald, who, after a spell at Cleethorpes where another of her sons was now domiciled, had returned to South Ferriby, the village of her birth. Great-Grandma Dawson, now in her late eighties, also lived in this North Lincolnshire village and, although not more than two years of age then, I can remember her white bonnet, wrinkled skin, and little cracked voice. She died before I was three, and was born in the year 1817, when Waterloo was still fresh in people's minds. In her childhood she must have known some folk who were alive at the time of Bonny Prince Charlie's rising in 1745. What an immense time span from then to the nineteen eighties.

In 1906, the centre of Hull was undergoing a "sea change"; if not into something rich and strange, it was certainly an improvement. The imposing new Alfred Gelder Street, replacing the labyrinth of narrow alleys, and providing a wide approach to the Drypool Bridge over the River Hull, was flanked by the newly built Guildhall and Law Courts on one side, and the new Head Post Office on the other. The post office was built on the site of the old Suffolk Palace, home in medieval times of the De la Pole family, who became Earls of Suffolk. These were the rich merchants who were largely

9

responsible for the little port of Wyke receiving royal favour from Edward I and becoming the town of Kingston-upon-Hull, with a royal charter, in 1299, William De la Pole receiving a knighthood and becoming the first mayor. On the south side of the post office, the quaintly named Bowlalley Lane recalls the time when it was the site of the bowling alley attached to the grounds of the Suffolk Palace. Opposite one end of Bowlalley Lane is Land of Green Ginger, a street whose title conjures up visions of medieval merchants buying and selling exotic wares brought to the port from the magical east.

High Street, not far away, was, up to Stuart times, the home of the town's gentry, and still maintains in spite of wartime bombing much of its earlier charm. Pride of place here must be given to Wilberforce House, an Elizabethan edifice, originally occupied by the Lister family, which later became famous as the birthplace of William Wilberforce, whose great work in and out of Parliament led to the abolition of the slave trade within the British Empire in the early part of the 19th century. The house, with its period furnishing, now houses many exhibits of the slave trade including sale bills, and the heavy manacles which the wretched slaves wore on their nightmare journeys in the slave ships across the Atlantic.

Another clutter of narrow streets up to 1906 blocked a direct route from Beverley Road to the Queen Victoria Square, and the electric tramway (only recently replacing the old horse-drawn trams) had to turn down Albion Street into Bond Street, its city terminus. The building of King Edward Street, cutting straight through to the Square, altered all that. I shall be coming back to the evolution of Hull later on, but in the meantime another chapter holding out exciting prospects to the Heald family was about to open.

CHAPTER TWO

In 1906 there was some disagreement between Guy and his technical staff over the future running of the firm and, after a good deal of thought, the partnership of Guy, Heald and Hearson was dissolved.

Dad, on his visits to South Ferriby and Ferriby Sluice, had seen ship-building potential in a small tidal creek situated to the east of the haven at Ferriby Sluice where the River Ancholme empties its water through a system of locks into the Humber estuary. The Ancholme had been canalised in earlier days, with the old river still meandering through the valley, its main purpose being now for drainage. The main waterway carried a good deal of commercial traffic between the market town of Brigg and the Humber ports in the square-rigged Humber keels and fore-and-aft rigged sloops, mostly operated by family owners. There were also several steam-driven barges, two of which, the *Togo* and *Swift*, come to my mind.

In addition to this, Ferriby Sluice and its jetty was the Lincolnshire terminal of the river packet service for goods and passengers which ran daily, Sundays excepted, between Sluice and Hull. This service was operated by the Goole and Hull Steam Packet Company, and during the next few years we were to get to know Captain Maltby and the ferrymen crew of *Her Majesty* very well indeed.

Dad, who needed financial backing for his venture, interested his uncle — Joseph Dawson — in the project. Uncle Joe, Grandma's youngest brother, had an interest in a number of farms in the area and, with his nephew Harold, ran a thriving butchery business. The idea of the shipyard appealed to him, and the requisite capital being forthcoming, the project began to take shape.

The creek was dredged and deepened, a dry dock was built, ancillary buildings including a steam sawmill were erected, and tools and equipment installed. Staff were engaged, with Joseph Tutty as foreman, others being a shipwright named Beresford, and a young labourer, Jack Howson.

In the meantime, mother was helping to clear up at 49 Sculcoates Lane, and early in 1907 the move to Ferriby Sluice took place. Initially we had a whitewashed cottage near the ferry terminal. The main things I remember about this cottage were its oak beams, and a knot hole in the floor of the children's bedroom through which Dorothy and I could hear conversations going on in the living room below. By putting an eye to the hole we could also get a restricted view of what was going on down there! I don't think our parents ever knew to what extent they were, in modern parlance, being "bugged."

Some time later we got possession of a bigger house, "Oakdene" it was called, on the Ferriby road. Here, I had a bedroom of my own, with a view from the window over miles of open country. I was not yet of school age, and

Ferry Sluice and River Ancholme (canal waterway to Brigg). 1909.

12

"Her Majesty" moored in Ferriby Sluice Haven. A Humber sloop passing in background. 1908.

13

when the shipyard opened I wandered where my fancy took me around the plant. Orders for ship repair work, mostly Humber keels, were coming in, and the new invoice and letter-heading paper — "J. T. Heald, Ship and Boat Builder, Marine Surveyor — Shipyard and Dry Dock, Ferriby Sluice, near Hull" — came into use.

Jack Howson of the shipyard staff had a younger brother, Charlie, a year older than I was, and we soon became boon companions. We enjoyed sharing meal breaks with the workmen, and spent many fascinating hours on the tideline. At times I was the despair of my mother, coming home with boots thick with mud, and sometimes trousers too, from venturing too far into the mud and wrack below high water mark.

One well-remembered occasion saw me in complete disgrace. A keel was in dry dock being fitted with new timbers, and the approach to the dock at one side was across a plank about ten feet long. Depending on the state of the tide, the plank crossed a stretch of mud, or several feet of water. On this occasion I was enjoying myself running across the plank and back again when my mother, who had walked over from the house for some reason or other, happened to see me. She stood petrified with fright, expecting any second to see me slip off and be engulfed in five or six feet of muddy water.

Then Dad came on the scene, sized up the situation, and quietly called to me to come ashore. This I did, and was completely mystified when I saw my mother in tears, and Dad looking very solemn. I got a good talking-to despite my protestations that I was never in the slightest danger of losing my balance! After that incident, crossing the plank without an escort was very definitely forbidden notwithstanding my mature age of four years.

I would sometimes wander along the bank of the River Humber and gaze across the two-mile stretch of water, watching the trains on the Yorkshire side. On a clear day it was possible to see their long plumes of steam and smoke as they sped along from Hull and Hessle. Just beyond North Ferriby Station the railway line passed through a belt of woodland. For a few seconds the white plumes were lost to sight, then they would re-appear and eventually be lost in the distance as the trains travelled to London or Leeds. I always hoped they were going to London, that fairytale place of which everybody spoke as being the centre of the world.

Less than half a mile off shore from Ferriby Sluice stood Read's Island, a flat green "holm" a mile and a half long, and half a mile wide. It was formed about two centuries ago by the build-up of mud and silt brought down from the Ouse and the Trent. The navigational passage for shipping going up the Humber to the river port of Goole on the Ouse was, at that time, to the south of Read's Island, and we used to get a close-up view of ships up to 2,000 tons navigating the passage between Ferriby Sluice and the island.

Shipping always came up-stream on the flood tide, and down-stream on the ebb. It was only possible for the bigger ships to get into Goole Docks at

The dry dock, with "Empress," the paddle steamer, in background, Read's Island beyond. It is here that I scared my parents crossing from shore to dock (age four).

the height of the tide. I can hear even now the "plonk! plonk!" of the screw propellers as the big ships passed on a calm summer's day only a couple of hundred yards from shore, their wash after they had passed creating a succession of big waves, thumping as they broke on the shore.

Beyond Sluice Bridge, on the road to Wintringham, the land is very low lying, and on the highest spring tides the road and the neighbouring fields would be flooded. Motor traffic in those days was practically non-existent, and carriers' carts, with other horse-drawn vehicles, could usually get through the foot or so of water which covered the road at these high tides. To aid direction, and to assist pedestrians who might be caught by the flooding, a series of switchbacks had been provided where stranded passengers could wait until the floods subsided as the tide receded. My sister Dorothy used to have nightmares, thinking that the flooding might reach our house. It never did, of course, as we were on slightly higher ground, so these fears were quite groundless.

With a nautical occupation, it was natural that my father should soon acquire a boat for sailing on the Humber, and the one he obtained was a converted ship's lifeboat with a removable mast. I can remember what a treat it was to go with him over to Read's Island and call on Mr. Kirby, who farmed cattle and sheep on the rich pasture. His family was the only one on the island, and in rough weather he had quite a problem on his hands ferrying the children across the water between the island and Sluice Haven en route to and from school.

Wild duck bred in large numbers in the reedy marshes round the island, and not infrequently a juicy duck and a dozen eggs from Read's formed an addition to our normal diet. At the end of the summer, huge flocks of pink-footed geese arrived from their breeding areas in Iceland and the far north of Europe, and made for the mudflats around Read's Island, to stay until the end of April. To see them arriving in "V"-shaped echelons, thousands and thousands of them, was indeed a sight, only matched by the hard metallic sounds of "Honk! Honk!" until the sky was filled with their reverberating cacophany.

As a change from Read's Island, we would occasionally sail across to the Yorkshire side of the Humber, and put in at Brough Haven. Brough was the headquarters of the Humber Yawl Club, and as Dad knew a number of their members, it was a chance to have a chat and an exchange of views on sailing matters.

Boating on the River Ancholme was equally pleasurable, but quite different. Once through the entrance locks, one was in gently flowing fresh water, gliding along between low banks with clusters of kingcups and other wild flowers. Here and there, a shady tree invited a mooring and a picnic followed by an afternoon nap. To the south-east, the Lincolnshire Wolds with their mosaic of fields and hedges, and clumps of trees on the nearer

16

skyline, faded into the distance. A couple of miles upstream was Horkstow suspension bridge, and a mile farther on was the picturesque stone bridge of Saxby. Each section had its interesting features until the limit of navigation beyond the market town of Brigg, ten miles away, was reached.

The old swing bridge (hand operated), Ferriby Sluice.

CHAPTER THREE

My father was never an angler — his hobbies were photography and sailing — but one of the features of life at Ferriby Sluice before the First World War was the annual Angling Festival and Water Carnival on the Ancholme, which brought in hundreds of fishermen and general visitors from a wide area. Many of them came from Hull, and the Packet Company had to augment their normal service on *Her Majesty* by bringing the *Empress* into temporary service. *Empress* usually plied between Hull and Goole, and this pair of paddle steamers was a familiar sight on the upper Humber.

Captain Maltby of *Her Majesty* knew every inch of the intricate approach, round a sandbank, into Ferriby Sluice Haven, and his ship was never known to foul the bank or run aground. I can see him now, a slightly greying, bearded figure, giving his orders through the speaking tube to his engine room. "Half speed ahead!" he would say, his eyes taking in the situation, against the challenge of a fast tide-race and that ominous sandbank. "Slow astern!" would follow, and the paddles slowly reversed as the steering wheel spun round. Then, "Full speed ahead!" was quickly followed by "Stop" and *Her Majesty* slowly — oh, so slowly — drew alongside and gently kissed the jetty, usually without a fender being required.

Captain Fleming's craft, the *Empress*, was a bigger boat than *Her Majesty* and his visits to Ferriby Sluice were of necessity somewhat spasmodic. Consequently, he had the utmost difficulty in navigating his ship alongside on half-tides (full tides were no problem), and on a number of occasions I have seen *Empress* go aground at the mouth of the Haven on a falling tide. In these cases, passengers had to be ferried ashore in small boats, or wait with whatever patience they had, until the flood tide lifted them off!

Over the years, we got to know Captain Maltby and his men on *Her Majesty* very well. The engineer was named Martin, and the purser was Fred Howson, elder brother of Jack and Charlie, my shipyard friends. Captain Maltby was a staunch Wesleyan and when at home never missed the morning service at South Ferriby Wesleyan Methodist Chapel.

My father had a pleasant tenor voice, and during the time we were at Sluice Shipyard he was joint superintendent of the Sunday School with his uncle (and my great-uncle) Joe Dawson. Dad had a talent for mimicry, an aptitude which I have to some extent inherited. Some of the local preachers, worthy characters, had idiosyncracies which to one with the necessary talent invited mimicry. Dad was a great favourite with Aunt Sally — one of the Dawson sisters — who had married Fred Twidle of Sluice Farm, and I have seen her in fits of laughter as Dad gave his impression of one or other of the local preachers, as we all sat in the comfortable farm parlour. I, too, would occasionally join in and add to the general merriment.

A family with whom we became friendly were the Straws. Frank Straw was the Ferriby Sluice lock-keeper, and was in charge of the arrangements for craft entering and leaving the River Ancholme. They had two children, young Frank of about my age, and his sister a year or so younger. Lock-keeper Frank was an authority on the river, its traffic, and its wild life. In constant touch as he was with incoming and outgoing vessels, he had his fingers on the pulse of all the local news and gossip. There was a swing bridge over the lock, worked by hand in those days, and favoured children were allowed to stand on the bridge when it was being opened for river traffic. I never heard of an accident, or any kind of incident involving the children, for Frank kept a very wary eye on the situation.

As a family, we were always welcome at Sluice Farm. Dad with his technical "know how" could usually find the odd job which required doing around the farm. He made an ornamental arch at the approach through the garden to the farmhouse, and this graced the entrance for many years.

Never have I tasted such delicious cool milk as came from the farm dairy, a cellar, approached down a flight of steps from a passageway in the house, and with a window just above ground level. Whenever Dorothy and I went to the farm Aunt Sally would say, "Now, children, would you like a glass of milk?" We never said no! They had a horse and trap, which was at our disposal if we wished to use it, and when the opportunity came we would go for a drive into the countryside. The pony was a handsome skewbald called "Laddie." The earliest outing I can remember was to the Twigmoor Gull Ponds, at Scawby near Brigg. We drove through Winterton, and along a section of Ermine Street, the old Roman Road which ran straight as an arrow from the Humber to Lincoln and beyond. Twigmoor was the nesting site of a big colony of black-headed gulls, and in the season nests were everywhere — it was difficult to walk around the perimeter of the ponds without treading on them. I still remember my astonishment when shown an egg with the chick in the act of pecking its way out.

Uncle Joe Dawson and Aunty Emmy lived at "Woodville" in South Ferriby. Here, the escarpment of the Lincolnshire Wolds drops away to the levels of the Ancholme valley, and from "Woodville" on the lower slopes of the hill range one had a superb view westward. Perhaps the most striking feature was the prospect of the upper Humber which curved in a deep arc between Ferriby and Whitton Ness. Neatly placed in the centre of the arc was Read's Island with its grazing sheep and cattle, and across the river to the north-west the Yorkshire Wolds continued the chalk range behind the villages of Welton, North Ferriby and Elloughton. I have heard it said that on a very clear day the towers of York Minster could be seen 35 miles away.

Just below South Ferriby village were the patchwork fields of the low-lying Ancholme valley, locally known as Carrs, with Sluice Mill showing up prominently, and the massed chimneys of the Scunthorpe iron and steel complex on the ridge of the Lincoln Heights beyond. A feature of the steel plant was the periodic opening of the furnaces, and when this occurred during the hours of darkness, a lurid glow lit up the sky for miles around. At first, Dorothy was terrified of this spectacle and took a lot of convincing that it was quite harmless.

In the summertime, "Woodville," with its terraced gardens, was a popular venue for church garden parties, and somehow the weather always seemed to be on its best behaviour on these occasions. The frilly Edwardian dresses, and large hats, of the ladies, were ideally suited for parasols, rather than umbrellas! Tea was served on the lawns, and there were the usual competitions like guessing the weight of a cake, hoop-la, and bowling for the prize of a cockerel.

Uncle Joe was a good mixer, had an infectious laugh and was usually in the centre of whatever fun was going. His wife, Aunty Emmy, had a quiet disposition and walked with the grace of a duchess. She played the organ at the Wesleyan Chapel, and was naturally a charming hostess at the garden parties. She was a member of the Stamp family of Barton-on-Humber who had been running a trans-Humber goods service since Stuart times. "Stamp's Boat" was a household term at Barton and on the Hull waterfront for many years. Their marriage was obviously the attraction of opposites, and their great disappointment was that they had no family. Consequently the numerous nephews and nieces were more to the fore than might otherwise have been the case.

Uncle Joe had a dogcart which I was to become more familiar with in later years, and also a pony and trap with a lively chestnut/black pony named "Gipsy." I remember going for a drive with them along the leafy Brigg road, when we passed a colony of rabbits disporting themselves in a field by the roadside near Saxby. I was obviously interested in their caperings, and Uncle Joe stopped the trap and said, "Why not go and see if you can catch one? Go for their tails, it's quite easy." So through the hedge I went and ran towards the nearest group. Naturally, they scampered away and disappeared down the rabbit-holes. So off I went to another group and the same thing happened. At length, disappointed and crestfallen, I walked back to the trap where Uncle Joe was trying to hide his chuckles. "You'll have to try again another time, Bernie," he said. "When you do, take some salt with you and see if you can scatter it on their tails, that'll get 'em." Although not yet quite five years old, I sensed that there was a catch somewhere, and didn't try again.

During this time, work at the shipyard as going ahead. Several repair jobs had been completed, but the big event was the building of a new lighter on a suitable site for an eventual launch, near the river bank. After the keel was laid, the ribs had to be sawn and bent to shape, and the screech of the sawmill was a familiar sound. For bending and shaping the ribs, a steam chamber was used, and the action of the hot steam on the oak timber soon

21

A family group at South Ferriby, 1907. Grandma Heald extreme left, Dad behind her. Dorothy and my mother next to Grandma, self holding Mum's knee. Alderman Joe Dawson extreme right (great uncle), near his wife, Aunt Emmie, sitting.

Uncle Joe Dawson with Aunt Emmie and 'Gipsy' at South Ferriby, 1909.

enabled the shipwrights to obtain the correct curves.

Later on, followed the caulking and decking. The caulking was done by hammering the okum, a tarry twisted fibre, into the joints of the planking — the okum was said to have been prepared by prisoners in the county gaols. One of the friendly shipwrights let me "have a go" at caulking, and I felt immensely proud to have had some part in the building of the ship. Needless to say, his brawny arm, tanned and tattooed, soon rammed home and completed my puny efforts.

At length, the day fixed for launching arrived. It was mid-September 1908, when my father judged the tide level to be right for the occasion. Sitting on its slipway, the lighter was decked from bow to stern in colourful bunting. Dorothy and I were attired in our Sunday best, and all the village gradually arrived to see the unusual spectacle of a launching. Dad had arranged for two of his men, both expert swimmers, to act as a temporary crew to man the vessel, and Dorothy, as the daughter of the shipbuilder, was to perform the launching ceremony.

A small staging had been erected for this purpose, and at the precise moment Dorothy swung the bottle of champagne against the hull of the vessel and called out, "I name this ship *Patience*. May God bless her, and all who sail in her." The chocks were knocked out, and *Patience* started to move down the greased slipway, gathering speed as she slid gracefully into the tidal waters below, accompanied by the cheers of the crowd watching the

"Patience" on the stocks. Dad Heald, Dorothy, the author, and three of the shipyard staff.

Dorothy christening "Patience." The author in sailor suit, Dad Heald on left. September, 1908.

proceedings. There was a feeling of relief among the launching party that everything had gone so well, and for Dorothy, who had been carefully rehearsed in her part, it was a red letter day which she was to remember with pride and pleasure for the rest of her life. No work was done after that, of course, and all concerned went off to celebrate for the remainder of the day.

Shortly after my fifth birthday on 20th December, 1908, and following the Christmas holidays, it was my turn to start attending school, a prospect which caused me some trepidation. Rather strangely, Dorothy, whom one would have judged to have had an aversion towards school, had taken a great liking to it very quickly after our arrival at Ferriby Sluice. The village children were friendly, and although the headmaster, Mr. Shrigley, had a reputation for standing no nonense, a twinkle was often to be seen in his eye. As this was a Church of England school, catechisms were taught, and the rector paid periodic visits.

The schoolmistress was a Miss Havercroft, and on my first morning when I was brought by my mother, accompanied of course by Dorothy, she soon made me feel at home. Charlie Howson, my boon companion of the shipyard days, had started school some months earlier, so I was assured of a playmate. One of the older girls named Clark acted as monitor and teacher's assistant. She was a good-looking fresh complexioned girl with fair wavy hair, and it was she who introduced the infants to the mysteries of the alphabet, getting to know the various letters, and making pot-hooks. We each had a slate and slate pencil — exercise books in primary schools were unheard of in those days — and it was a simple matter to wipe the slate clean for the next exercise.

The playground was a small paved yard, but the bigger boys had an area outside the playground proper, where they were able to work off their surplus energy in the games popular at the time. The playground had a low wall with a coping which had been rounded by generations of children and their trousers. We infants used to sit astride the wall at intervals, each hopping along and trying to catch up the one ahead, a sort of follow-my-leader. The girls, of course, had very different ideas for games.

A number of children had long distances to come to school, one family named Clarvis with several members of school age having to walk about three miles from an outlying farm on the Winteringham road. For my sister and me the walk was a mere mile!

CHAPTER FOUR

By the spring of 1909 it was realised that our halcyon days at Ferriby Sluice were drawing to a close. Repair work at the shipyard was difficult to get, and not sufficient to keep the yard fully occupied, while no further orders for new craft were forthcoming. The enterprise was running at a loss, and it was obvious that to avoid bankruptcy the shipyard would have to close down. Perhaps with additional capital, more publicity, and better salesmanship methods, it might have been possible to carry on — I don't know.

One thing is certain. If the yard had been working five years later when the 1914-18 war broke out, the place would have been humming with activity. With the struggle for survival in those years, new shipping of all kinds was vital, and there is no doubt that Ferriby Sluice Shipyard would have been working to capacity, with a consequent lifting of our financial fortunes. But it was not to be, and two years before the outbreak of that war the Heald family was to suffer a deadly blow on another front.

However, that was in the future, and my father's first priority was to find a suitable job where his skills would bring some reward, or at any rate a living. After some searching, this turned out to be a position as supervising foreman with the Hull Ship Repairing and Dry Dock Company, whose premises were in High Street, Hull. A house had to be found and various localities in the Hull perimeter were explored to find something suitable.

A repair job in the dry dock. Dad in the picture. 1909.

The search was narrowed to the Holderness Road area, and eventually one was found which fulfilled requirements at a reasonable rental in Lee Street. No. 34 was the first of a new development of three-bedroomed houses backing on to open fields beyond which was the East Park. We moved house in late July, a sad business for us all, as we had loved living in Lincolnshire. *Her Majesty* conveyed us from the Sluice Jetty for the last time as local residents, down the river to Hull Corporation Pier, and it was to be the last cruise on the old paddle steamer for some time.

Our house in Lee Street contrasted greatly with "Oakdene" at Ferriby Sluice. Instead of the oil lamps which had to be trimmed and filled regularly, we now had gas for illumination and cooking. Gas mantles gave a brilliant white light, but were very fragile. The gas brackets needed only a slight knock for the mantle to disintegrate, leaving just a blue flame like a bunsen burner. As we children grew older, and a bout of skylarking with Dad happened to develop, a gas mantle was a not infrequent casualty, and mother would say, "Lawk-a-massy! There's another mantle gone."

Whereas in Lincolnshire our ablutions had to be taken in a hip bath, now we had a full-length bath situated in the back kitchen. Hot water was not installed until some time later, and bath water was heated with the aid of a gas heater about four feet long under the bath. The snag with this was that if one got in too soon after the heat was turned off, one got up again very quickly! I can remember very vividly the shock of one's bottom coming into contact with the hot metal of the bath, and the "Ouch!" which followed.

One big improvement over the house at Ferriby Sluice was the flush toilet. Gone was the old "country seat" and I was most intrigued by this example of urban amenities, taking every opportunity, until the novelty wore off, of pulling the chain and hearing the swish and watching the swirl of water as the cistern did its work. We had a telephone installed so that Dad could be in touch with his firm out of hours — dry docking was dependent on the state of the tide, as the dock gates could only be opened or closed to allow the passage of shipping at or near high water, and this could happen during the night hours. Our telephone was on a four-party line, the number being 555X4, and an incoming call was announced by the bell ringing in all four houses, one long and a series of shorts, ours being one long and four shorts, denoting the . . .X4. This seems a cumbersome system by modern standards, but was up to date at that time, and a normal practice with party lines.

Our garden was miniscule compared with the rural one, but reasonable enough by urban standards. One big advantage was the open field behind the garden, and beyond that, Hull's biggest park. The open area of grass where children could play at will was to remain with us for three or four years, until another street of houses, Summergangs Road, blocked our view of the park.

One of the first things my parents had to settle was the question of

28

Lee Street, Hull, about 1912. Our house was the one with the upper bay near the lamp post on the right. Vicarage garden fence, scene of one of our exploits, on left.

schooling. In a rapidly growing area, accommodation was tight, and the result was that Dorothy, now twelve years old, started after the summer holidays at Estcourt Street School, while I, still not six, had to go to Mersey Street. Both schools, though in different directions, were slightly less than a mile away frorm home. I can't say that my days at Mersey Street School were particularly happy ones. The school was situated in a thickly populated working class area, and the classes were crowded. Many of the children were far from clean and obviously came from very poor families, some of them coming regularly to school barefoot. There was also a bullying element which didn't help me to settle down.

A source of interest to me were the street gas lamps. Shortly before dark, a small army of lamplighters went the rounds carrying poles containing a paraffin torch, and lighting each lamp in turn, street by street. After the total darkness in the country when daylight had gone, this was a great change. At school on winter afternoons — we did not leave until 4 p.m. — one of the staff would come round with a long taper to light the gas mantles.

By the time 1910 came in, we were settling down in our new surroundings, and a few words about life in the last year of the Edwardian Era might be appropriate. Motor cars were few and far between, and the hansom cab was the city man's and the doctor's mode of transit. For the rest of us the electric trams provided a convenient means of getting to the town centre along Holderness Road, the fare being a penny all the way for adults and a ha'penny for children. The trams were open ended, the drivers and conductors being exposed to the elements, and in rainy weather drivers clad in sou'westers and oilskins looked as if they might have stepped straight out of Grace Darling's lifeboat.

I remember one grey-bearded old driver — he must have been approaching his retirement — who was quite a character. On one occasion a grocer's errand boy pushing a tricycle piled with groceries had the misfortune to see his goods topple into a heap on the roadway, just as our friend was arriving on the scene with his tram. Surveying the wreckage where burst bags of flour and sugar mingled with broken eggs, he called out, "Now, me lad, what are you trying to do, make a pudding?"

Soon after 10 o'clock at night the trams were safely tucked in the sheds at Aberdeen Street, and for the next hour or so it was the turn of the private enterprise covered-wagonettes to reap a harvest from the people spending an evening with friends in the suburbs, or returing from town centre entertainments. As they stood outside "Mile House" (now the Crown Hotel) near East Park, the wagonette drivers' shouts of "town way up" would be heard echoing in the streets.

During the day, the "clop! clop!" of horses' hooves was constantly heard as the various trades and service vehicles came round the streets. The milkman would come down from his float and, calling out "Milk!" in a loud voice, would fill the housewives' jugs from his huge can, ladling out the milk with his pint measure, and usually exchanging a bit of chaffing with his customer. "Washing out early today, Mrs! Couldn't you sleep?" or perhaps, "My, that's a good smell," sniffing the aroma of baking, "Somebody's birthday?"

Then there was the coalman with his rully, calling out "Coal! Coal!" or "Gas-house cin*ders*!" with voice raised and accent on the "ders." Household nuts were 10d per bag, and there were sixteen bags to the ton in Hull, not twenty as in most places. Best coal was 1/- or 1/1d per bag, depending on the colliery which had produced the coal, Sharlston being generally regarded as the top quality coal. The greengrocer had his regular round, mainly for those people who found it difficult to get to the shops, charging a copper or two more for the convenience of delivery. Even so, prices were ridiculously low by present standards, eating apples and pears being 2d per pound, perhaps even 1/- a stone, while good quality Spanish oranges in the season were three for a penny, or even four from market stalls.

With so many horse-drawn vehicles around, there was no difficulty in obtaining manure for the gardens. One simply took a bucket and shovel, and collected what one required from the street. The corporation, however, did employ "orderly boys" who went round the streets and thoroughfares pushing high-sided barrows equipped with brushes, shovels, and buckets. Their job was to sweep up the horse droppings, and generally keep the streets clean and tidy. The boys wore a smart blue uniform with tippy cap, and for those school leavers who didn't go for an apprenticeship, or into an office, an orderly boy's job was considered quite a good one and usually led to a position as a permanent member of the corporation staff. Some were content to settle for refuse collecting, others graduated to the Parks Department as gardeners.

In a street where the houses were all very much alike, there was a covered passageway for each two houses. This led to the back door, a concreted yard, and so to the house. On one occasion during our first months in Lee Street, I was running home after playing in the street, and turned into the wrong passage. The door was ajar, and I ran across the yard and into the kitchen. I realised I was in the wrong dwelling when I saw the lady of the house having a "good wash" stripped to the waist at the kitchen sink! This was the first time I had seen a bare female torso, and my astonishment and embarrass-ment must have shown in my face. "Hullo, ducky!" she said, as I stared open-mouthed, "You've make a mistake, and come into the wrong house." She said this with a smile, and showed her presence of mind in so doing, as most women would have shouted in annoyance. I muttered something which was meant for an apology and quickly ran out of the house thinking deeply. But I never made the same mistake again.

31

CHAPTER FIVE

1910 was the year of the two elections, one in January and one in December. The reigning Member of Parliament for East Hull was Thomas Robinson Ferens, a Liberal. He was also an ardent churchman, and the superintendent of the Brunswick Wesleyan Sunday School, which Dorothy and I had started to attend.

Hull was a Liberal stronghold in those days, two of its three constituencies being Liberal held. The Labour Party was still in its infancy, and straight fights were the order of the day — Liberal v. Conservative. Two elections in one year were almost too good to be true as far as we children were concerned. My family were staunch Liberals, and as the majority of my new school-friends' families were of similar persuasion, it was to be expected that we should wear the orange favours.

We had great fun as the election day drew near, going around in bands singing:

"Vote, vote, vote for Mr. Ferens,
You can't vote for a better man,
Mr. Ferens is the man,
And we'll have him if we can,
And we'll throw old Monte in the dock!"

"Monte" was the nickname of Mr. Sebag Montefiore, the Conservative candidate. When Mr. Ferens retained his seat at both elections with comfortable majorities, our youthful enthusiasm reached great heights.

That year was a red letter one for our family in quite another direction. Early on April 18th, the family doctor came to the house in his hansom cab, mother having "not been well" that morning, and staying in bed for the day. Later in the day, Dad came to where I was playing in the garden and said, "Bernie, you've got a baby brother, would you like to see him?" Now, this was great news. Having a sister six years my elder, I was very much the junior partner, and this seemed a golden chance for a male alliance.

I was taken upstairs to the front bedroom, and there was my mother sitting up in bed with a baby snuggled in her arms. This was Joseph Dennis. I must admit I wasn't too impressed with him, for he had a very red face and wispy tousled hair, but as this was my first introduction to a new-born baby, I could perhaps be excused for some disappointment. I think I half expected to see a bouncing mature infant of about six months old, instead of the tiny bundle of humanity helpless in his mother's arms. However, my disappointment didn't last long, and Dennis proved a happy healthy child.

It was about this time that newspaper reports suggested that the king was not in good health. He had contracted a chill while staying at Biarritz, and this could not be shaken off. Medical bulletins were issued regularly, and the newspapers gave up-to-date reports of his progress, or lack of it. Then one morning, a newsboy came down the street at an unusual hour, and Dad thought he was shouting "Health of the King," but as he drew nearer we realised that he was shouting "Death of the King."

Everybody dashed out to buy a paper to scan the headlines, and read the solemn announcement that the king had indeed died, and that George V was king in his place. The date was May 6th, so baby Dennis could claim to have been born an Edwardian by a matter of eighteen days. The short reign of Edward VII — the Peacemaker — had come to an end at the age of 69. But as he himself had said when he was proclaimed king on the death of his mother, Queen Victoria, in 1901, "Sixty is a bit old to be finishing serving one's apprenticeship."

The death of Edward the Seventh was really the end of an epoch, the Edwardian days having been a somewhat graceful continuation of Victorian days with their gas lamps and cabbies, but also with their extremes of riches and poverty. Lloyd George's budget of 1909, which brought in a pension of 5/- per week for old people over 70 years of age, was a foretaste of the greater social equality to come in the days ahead, but they were yet far distant. I remember that my maternal grandparents, Grandpa and Grandma Hollingworth living at the other side of the city, found this little extra income of great value in their struggle to make ends meet.

Grandpa Hollingworth's sight was extremely poor. He had contracted glaucoma some years previously, and this had resulted in the complete loss of one eye. There was some sight in the other, but this was only retained by the daily application of drops, administered by Grandma. Their eldest son, Uncle Tom, a joiner employed in the wagon repair shops of the North Eastern Railway, and a bachelor until well on in life, lived with them. They occasionally visited us, when Grandpa liked nothing better than to get into a comfortable chair with the "Daily News" which, with A. G. Gardiner as editor, was the popular Liberal daily of the time. Grandpa could just manage to read the newsprint with the aid of a magnifying glass. He had a habit of whispering aloud what he was reading, and I used to watch him and wonder why he did it. I once discreetly asked my mother, and she said, "Oh, it's nothing, Bernie, only a little habit. Don't draw attention to it."

Sailor suits were very much the fashion for little boys at this time, and when my parents took me to an outfitters in the city centre to get one for me, I was quite excited. The one chosen for me was a good fit, and on putting my hand in one of the pockets while trying it on in the shop, I found a new sixpence there. This was great fun, and I said to the shopkeeper, "Do you always put money into a pocket when you sell a suit?" "Well, not always," he replied, "You are one of the lucky ones."

I couldn't wait to get home before really trying the suit out, and when I was at last able to run around in it, I felt on top of the world. The trousers were knee-length shorts, and the blouse had the regulation Nelson touch,

33

Dennis, Dorothy, and myself and new sailor suit, complete with lanyard and whistle. 1911.

with the three blue and white stripes on the collar. Best of all, was the lanyard complete with whistle, with which I was able to summon up the crew of *H.M.S. Victory* whenever I felt like it. The family must have been very tolerant to put up with the noise of the whistle until the novelty to some extent wore off.

Features of those days, which disappeared with the outbreak of the First World War, were the street musicians, including the German Bands, and the Dancing Bears. The German Bands were groups of itinerant musicians who performed mainly on stringed instruments, as far as I can recollect — I used to call them "scrapers." One group used to perform in Central Hull around the Charles Street/Fountain Road area, and I can remember their doleful expressions as their wailing instruments emitted what was in all probability good classical music, but this was long before I had any appreciation of Beethoven or Brahms.

A familiar figure in the streets of East Hull in those days was a blind man named Ellis. He used to walk up one street and down the next, singing and accompanying himself on a concertina. He had quite a good baritone voice and a remarkably big repertoire of songs. It was almost uncanny the way he knew how to keep clear of obstructions, and to recognise when he had reached a street corner and to make the required turn. Some sort of sixth sense in him must have been extremely active. He was married to a blind woman, and the pair of them had a stand on Saturdays outside the covered market near Holy Trinity Church in the Old Town. I should imagine his talents proved quite lucrative — his money box always seemed to be pretty well filled, and he was so well-known. "Morning, Mr. Ellis. How are you? Nice to see you again," was the sort of greeting he was constantly getting.

Another familiar figure was a little old lady usually clad in a bonnet, frilly dress, and a spotlessly white pinafore, who played a barrel organ at week-ends at the approach to either Drypool Bridge or North Bridge over the River Hull. Here she could catch the groups of people from East Hull wending their way city-wards for an afternoon or evening out.

Then there were the hurdy-gurdies twanging out the latest musical hits. Although they did their tours of the streets from time to time, their usual stands were outside the public houses, where sometimes they might be joined by one or two women — fortified by what they had imbibed — who would give a sort of Edwardian floor show with kicked up heels and twirling skirts. There were also the buskers who operated alongside the queues waiting to get into the Alexandra, Grand, and Palace theatres; from the one-man bands to the not-over-tuneful violinists. I remember one picture postcard sent to us about that time which showed two buskers, one operating his hand organ, and his female companion apparently singing lustily. He is saying to her, "Steady on Maria! Come down a notch, not so much like Patti, more like Clara Butt!"

The Dancing Bears were in a different category. They were aimed principally at juvenile audiences, and most of the animals were well trained and extremely docile, although children were warned not to bait or irritate them. Their tricks had obviously had plenty of rehearsal, and groups of us would stand fascinated as the animals did their stuff and then wait for their reward of sugar lumps from the owner's pocket.

CHAPTER SIX

Holidays for the lower-middle and working classes prior to 1914 usually consisted of odd days at the seaside, or rooms in an apartment house where the family on holiday provided the food which was prepared and cooked by the landlady, or yet again a furnished house. As we had only moved from Ferriby Sluice during the summer of 1909, holidays for that year were out. The following year, however, with Dad having a steady income, the question of holidays cropped up.

People living in Hull had, and still have, a wide selection of seaside resorts within easy range. The favourites for the rank and file were Cleethorpes over the Humber in Lincolnshire, and Withernsea and Hornsea on the Holderness coast. Bridlington, and particularly Scarborough, "Queen of Watering Places," were for the better off. All the Yorkshire resorts had rail communications with Hull, and fares were amazingly cheap, ranging from 1/- return to Hornsea and Withernsea, to 2/6 and 3/- to Bridlington and Scarborough. Our choice was Withernsea, where we secured rooms in Cheverton Avenue, only a few yards from the sea front. We chose Withernsea partly because of its reputation for bracing air, and partly because we were handily placed, living in East Hull, for Southcoates Station on Holderness Road which was one of a number of suburban stations on the line from the central Paragon Station before reaching open country.

Alas, both the Withernsea and Hornsea lines were closed under the Beeching axe years later, and Hull's famous — or infamous — level crossings are now only a memory, with the exception of Spring Bank West on the Bridlington line. Road bridges were built after World War Two over the main line railway where it crossed Anlaby and Hessle Roads, cutting out the worst of the level crossing delays.

In passing, the possibility of a Humber Bridge was talked about in my childhood over sixty years ago, and between the wars I remember attending a popular concert at the Hull Queen's Hall when the variety artiste "Stainless Stephen" was on the bill. Apologising for being late because of a lengthy hold-up (!) at one of the level crossings, he said, "People of Hull, I have the ideal solution for your level crossing problems, and it would cost very little. Would you like to hear what it is?" "Yes," yelled the audience. "All you have to do," said Stainless, "Is to take up your level crossings, place them end to end across the Humber, and you have your Humber Bridge and solve the level crossing problems at a stroke."

But to return to the holidays. Mother's cousins, the Turners, had two children who were of similar age to Dorothy and myself, and were also going to Withernsea for their holiday, so naturally we joined forces. They had visited us several times at Ferriby Sluice, and we were all on very friendly terms.

36

Although I was familiar enough with the Humber, this was my first visit to the real sea, and I found it tremendously exciting. Whether we had any rain, I can't remember, the holiday seemed to be one long succession of glorious days on the beach with bucket and spade, or paddling around in the pools near the groins. Being six years of age, I went to bed quite early in the evenings, and one recollection is of lying in bed with the window wide open, and hearing someone next door playing on the piano and singing, "*Summer suns are glowing over land and sea.*" As I dropped off to sleep it seemed like a touch of heaven, and that hymn has ever since been one of my favourites.

This was the time when the popularity of the Pierrots was at its height, and Will Catlin from Scarborough had a company playing at Withernsea. They were part of the seaside scene, and although I was too young to follow most of their quips, the songs and sketches were enjoyed by grown-ups and children alike.

It was in connection with the Pierrots that I witnessed my first scene of crowd violence, extremely mild though it was by present-day standards. The Withernsea Council had decided to erect barriers across the normally free promenade when the evening performance was due, and charge admission. This thoroughly incensed the holiday crowd, and on this occasion they took the law into their own hands, overturned the barriers and poured through to have a free session, apart from the normal collection taken up by one of the Pierrots. This incident happened on the last evening of our holiday, and I was allowed to stay up later than usual, otherwise I should have missed the excitement. I never heard what the outcome was, but the local council had made themselves very unpopular.

At this time, bathing machines were still in existence, although on the way out, and were being replaced by tents and huts above high water mark. I expect the bathing machines with their steps, pushed into the waves by attendants, were used by the modest and ageing representatives of the Victorian Age.

Regretfully, we had to pack away our buckets and spades, shrimping nets, and all the other holiday paraphernalia, and catch the train back to Hull again. Apart from our annual holiday we had the odd day at Hornsea, where the sea had a counter-attraction in the fresh water mere. Reed-fringed Hornsea Mere, besides being the largest natural fresh water lake in Yorkshire, was the home of many varieties of water fowl, of which Canada geese, mallards and great crested grebes come to mind. It was well stocked with fish, and a popular haunt for the owners of small sailing craft. Towards the close of a summer evening, with the sun dipping over its western end and sending a shimmering pathway over the water, Hornsea Mere is a place to linger over and reflect.

The following year, Dorothy and myself spent a few days with Dad's brother Joe and his wife, who lived at Cleethorpes. Joe Heald had a master plumber's business on the outskirts of Grimsby, and his wife was a well-known music teacher in Grimsby for many years. On one occasion Uncle Joe took Dorothy and me to an entertainment where the "joy wheel" was one of the attractions. This was a circular wooden disc or floor, about ten feet in diameter, positioned an inch or two above main floor level on a spindle or axis. When the power was applied, the disc began to revolve slowly, but gradually gained speed. Competitors from the audience were invited to take up their positions on the board before revolving started, and the winner was the one who could stay on the longest as the joy wheel gradually worked up speed. The surface was well polished, and the centrifugal force engendered meant that sooner or later everybody slid off at a tangent, to the amusement and delight of the onlookers. Those who took up positions nearer the centre obviously had a better chance of staying on longer than those near the edge.

On this occasion, Uncle Joe took Dorothy and myself on, and we children waited in some trepidation for the fun to begin. It was a peculiar sensation to feel oneself start to go round and round, and it wasn't long before first myself, and then Dorothy, slid off on to the carpet. Uncle Joe, however, was determined to show what he could do, and he grimly hung on as one and then another of the competitors slid off, until to our delight he was the last one to succumb, and was declared the winner. He was a great favourite with us children, and not having a family of his own, we probably came in for more of his attention. He smoked cigars, and whenever I smell the fragrance of a good cigar I am reminded of happy days at Cleethorpes before the First World War.

At that time, the Humber crossing between Hull Corporation Pier and New Holland was maintained by the paddle steamers *Cleethorpes* and *Grimsby* which had sometimes earlier replaced the *Doncaster* and *Sheffield*, two ancient 19th century boats. They were owned by the Great Central Railway whose Lincolnshire terminal was New Holland Pier, reaching out well into the river. They had the distinctive black and white funnels of the G.C.R., and were themselves replaced about 1912 by the *Brocklesby* and *Immingham*. It was on the latter that King George V and Queen Mary cruised down the Humber after opening Hull's newest and biggest dock, King George Dock, in 1914. But we are jumping the gun, as this was still in the future.

There used to be a catch question asked of strangers to the area. It was, "Where can one see a train leave one station, walk down the line, and catch it again at the next?" The answer was "New Holland Pier." The next station was New Holland Town at the other end of the pier, and it was a comparatively simple matter to walk along the pathway by the line side — incidentally getting good views up and down the river — and join the same train at the Town Station where it stayed long enough to be caught up by a good walker.

Children in Hull and East Yorkshire generally have for generations eagerly anticipated Hull Fair, which was always ceremoniously opened by the Mayor (after 1914, "Lord Mayor") each October 11th, and lasted a week. It was immediately preceded by Nottingham Goose Fair, and for years each of these cities claimed that theirs was the biggest fair in the country. The probability is that they were about equal in size and drawing power, and showmen from all over the country gathered for these big occasions.

My first visit was in 1909, when I was not quite six. The main approach to the fairground was down Walton Street, off Anlaby Road, and during Fair Week the Corporation trams ran a shuttle service to Walton Street from the city centre, these particular trams being marked "Fair Only." On this occasion my father and mother, with Dorothy and myself, went on a family outing, and excitement grew as we left the tram, and turned down Walton Street. It was early evening, already dusk, but the lights from the fairground cast a lurid glow over the city which could be seen for miles.

Walton Street was lined with stalls on both sides, each having a flaring paraffin lamp for illumination. There was everything to tempt the fair-goer to part with his money before he even reached the fair proper. There were stalls selling dishes of whelks and winkles, others selling candy floss, hot peas, brandysnap, and ice cream. Interspersed were fortune tellers — "The one and only Gipsy Lee," "The original Gipsy Rose Lee," "Gipsy Smith" — there they all were, swarthy and mysterious looking, as they sat at the entrance to their sanctums. Now and again a young couple would pause, and the girl would say to her companion with a self-conscious giggle, "Go on, George, let's have a go, and see what's in store for us," and they would disappear behind the curtain. One wondered what stories of romantic adventure or crosses to bear would be conjured up from the crystal ball or the lined palm.

Eventually we reached the fairyland of the fairground itself, and joined the jostling throng. Pride of place went to the round-abouts with their flying horses and their steam organs playing light classical music like *Zampa* or *Poet and Peasant*. A delightful sound it was, now, more's the pity, superseded by cacophonous electronically magnified horrors churning out the latest hit parade wailings. But in 1909-10 these were decades into the future as were the glaring neon lamps, so different from the mellow, low-powered electric bulbs, and the paraffin flares of the years before the First World War.

After a "go" on one of the smaller children's round-abouts, we all went into the long narrow tent containing the toy bazaar, and it was here that I experienced my first panic. The bazaar was packed with people, and I became separated from my parents and sister. Suddenly, I realised that I was lost — utterly lost among this seething crowd of humanity — and that I should never see my family again. Stifling a sob, I wriggled to and fro, dwarfed and in danger of being trampled upon by the almost solid wall of grown-ups. How long this lasted I don't know, but somehow I must have fought my way towards the exit, or been carried along by the continuous movement of the crowd, for I suddenly heard Dad say, "Bernie, there you are, we were beginning to think we had lost you." What a welcome sound, and what a joyful reunion! "You must keep hold of my hand now," said Dad, "And everything will be all right."

Since those days, I have occasionally seen little lost children in big stores or at the seaside being comforted by an attendant or passer-by, and I have been able to sympathise with and understand that dreadful loneliness and sickness of heart, for I have experienced it myself.

Well, after this incident, Dad thought it was time we had some refreshment — what was it to be, hot peas, chips, or Merrill's ice cream? We chose the ice cream. Now, during those early years of the century, G. P. Merrill, a stocky bearded figure, had built up a local reputation for his ice cream, which had a delicious distinctive flavour, unlike any other brands on sale at the time. He had also launched into the manufacture and preparation of custard powder, which when served up as custard, had the same delicious flavour as the ice cream. Imagine then, our satisfaction and my delight to sit down at a table in G. P. Merrill's tent, and consume a generous helping of ice cream garnished with custard — food for the Gods!

Later on, we peered at the draw curtains of some of the side shows, the fat lady with pictures showing her enormous thighs and blancmange-like bosom, the Siamese Twins, the Tiniest Couple Breathing, and the cat with two heads. Dad did not let us go in to see any of these freaks, or go into the boxing booth to see Champion Charlie take on all comers.

We did, however, go into the huge booth containing Bostock and Wombwell's Menagerie. The smell of the animals was a bit off-putting at first, but we got used to it, and I gazed in wonder at the magnificent tigers with their smouldering eyes, the rather bored-looking lions, the chattering monkeys, and the tiny Shetland pony which walked easily under a Great Dane dog. We stayed for Captain Wombwell's act, when he made the lions go through their performance, flicking his whip now and then at a recalcitrant animal and getting a growling response, until he achieved the grande finale of a disciplined grouping. Dad pointed out that throughout all the weaving and positioning of the animals, Captain Wombwell never turned his back on them.

At the end of the performance, it was time for us to make our way out of the fair to the waiting trams on Anlaby Road. But before we left the fairground, just beyond the lights and the pulsating activity, we paused to have a quick look at the ranks of the showmen's caravans, with children's faces peeping over the half-doors, and the odd glimpse of women at their chores inside, their faces lit up in the mellow light of the oil lamps.

A popular book at that time, at any rate in our part of the country, was *A Peep Behind the Scenes*, by Mrs. O. F. Walton. It gave a fascinating insight into the life of a showman's family, and part of the setting was at Hull Fair. After our visit to the Fair, Mother used to read extracts to us from the book as bedtime reading, and we used to sit entranced as the story unfolded.

CHAPTER SEVEN

In most respects, 1911 was a happy year for our family. We had the usual festivities at Christmas 1910 and over the New Year. Family parties were very much the thing, and favourite visitors to us were my mother's younger brother, Joe Hollingworth and his wife Hilda. Joe had a good baritone voice, Aunt Hilda was an expert pianist and could also sing contralto, while Dad was as mentioned earlier a tenor, and Mother was a soprano. All had had choir experience at the old Scott Street Methodist Chapel in their pre-marriage days, so vocal quartettes were popular, and such favourites as *Sweet and Low, O Who Will O'er the Downs with Me*, and *Juanita* were often sung. These visitors were sometimes reinforced by the Watson family, Joe, Annie and their son Harold from Otley in Wharfedale, old friends of the family, and on this occasion the Watsons stayed with us over Christmas. Joe and Annie were also good singers, and with all this talent available, a musical evening was bound to be a success.

Young Dennis was now a bouncing baby of eight months, and was much admired by the visitors for his good looks and sturdy frame. Harold Watson, who was of a mechanical turn of mind, was thirteen years old, and had received one of the early Mechano sets for a Christmas present. I delighted in "helping" him to build cranes, bridges, bogies, and all the other models which the Mechano construction sets were able to offer the budding engineer.

One of my presents was a wrought iron hoop, which Dad had had specially made for me by a local blacksmith. Most hoops were laminated wooden ones, and they only needed to be left out in the rain once or twice to begin to warp. This, though, was different. Instead of a wooden stick for propulsion, it had a foot long iron stave with a hook at the end. Once the hoop had started rolling, a light touch with the hook would either accelerate or retard the "vehicle" at will.

When the days lengthened, I used to run for miles with it in the East Hull suburbs, and I took a delight in steering it on a straight course. A flick of the wrist, and I passed a slow-moving pedestrian, another flick and I was away round the street corner on another long straight. The hum of iron on pavement was sweet music. That hoop was my magic carpet: one day it would be a motor car and I the driver; the next, it was a ship and I the navigator, charting the narrow seas of streets, and then venturing into the ocean of the main Holderness Road. The beauty of it was that I could return to port anytime I felt like it!

Dad had bought a bicycle which he found useful for getting around the area, and one day in the spring he said to me, "Would you like to come with me for a run to Paull on Saturday? I can take you on my crossbar." "Yes, please," I replied, with a nice feeling of anticipation. Paull is a village on

Humberside, six or seven miles east of Hull, at a point where the estuary takes a south-easterly turn. At that time a good deal of inshore fishing was done from the village, Paull shrimps and Humber smelts having a big local reputation, and river pollution was then minimal.

It was also the site of the Humber Defence Headquarters, Paull Battery being situated on the only hill in the vicinity, actually a glacial moraine left from the last Ice Age. It had a commanding position with an unobstructed view up and down river. The day Dad had chosen for our visit turned out to be also the day when the Territorial Artillery were doing firing exercises there. We went via Southcoates Lane on to Hedon Road, through Marfleet to the ancient little town of Hedon. There, we had a leg-stretcher, and looked in the beautiful old church known as the "King of Holderness." Then through the winding lanes to Paull itself, where we found the place thronged with visitors.

We took up a position on the slope of the hill, ate the picnic lunch which mother had packed, and waited for what was to follow.

The Territorials had manned the gun emplacements, and soon a tug came down stream towing a line of rafts with what looked like square canvas sails. These were the targets. When they came within the sights of the battery the guns opened up with an ear-splitting roar, and one could see holes appearing in the target sails, and spouts of water around the target area. A repeat performance followed as the flotilla swung round, and after several more salvoes the exercise was over. One presumes that notes were made of the accuracy achieved, and approval or otherwise passed to the gun crews. It was a peculiar experience for me, and my main memory is not of the shooting, but of the calm beauty of the sunlit scene as the targets sailed slowly past, half a mile or so out on the River Humber.

On another occasion Dad took me to see the work in progress on Hull's newest dock at Marfleet on Hedon Road, and jointly owned by the North Eastern and Hull and Barnsley Railway Companies. "Joint" Dock was not finished until three years later in 1914 and when we saw it the excavations were in progress with bogies and trollies removing thousands of cubic yards of earth from what would be the dock basin. Dad was particularly interested in the graving dock at the eastern end of the area. This was taking shape, and I marvelled at the vertical depth of this huge dry dock chasm. We peered over the edge, and I was glad to have my father's hand to hold as we gazed down to where the workmen were busy below.

The highlight of 1911, nationally, was the coronation of King George V and Queen Mary on 22nd June. At Hull, the celebrations included processions and fire-work displays, while every schoolchild received a gift of six new halfpennies in a special box. The coins, of course, were the first issue bearing the head of the new monarch. The really big event, though, was the visit to the Humber of a squadron of the Home Fleet of the Royal Navy.

Now, one of the features of the scene from the Corporation Pier for many years prior to 1914 was H.M.S. *Southampton,* a ship of the line from Nelson's time. This relic of the days of the "Wooden Walls of Old England" was used as a kind of floating reformatory, or training school for delinquent boys. Here, they were subjected to strict discipline, but were taught rowing and seamanship in general. To see a liberty boat coming ashore over the few hundred yards of water, with the officer in charge standing astern, and the boys rowing with clock-work precision, was a great sight. The majority of the boys involved eventually made successful careers in the Royal Navy, or Mercantile Marine.

During the naval visit, I was taken by my father to view the scene from the Pier. When darkness arrived, the fleet squadron, which was decked overall with bunting, became a sight from fairyland. The lights were suddenly switched on, and the outline of each ship, with H.M.S. *Southampton* in the foreground, was picked out in hundreds of electric bulbs. There they all were, in line, and a fine sample of Britain's sea power, stretching down river towards Grimsby. The fleet was indeed "lit up."

The coronation must have been a boost to industry, as the features of King George V and Queen Mary appeared on many articles in the shops from household linen to pint mugs and chocolate tins. We had a tin of chocolates bearing the picture of the Royal Family, from the new Prince of Wales down to Prince John, the youngest member, who died a few years later, while still only a child. This tin was used for keeping odds and ends in, long after the chocolates had disappeared.

Living so near as we were to Hull's East Park, it was natural that we should spend some of our leisure time there. The park had a thriving Model Yacht Club, based on a specially built pond, and with a clubhouse where the members were able to store their yachts when not in use. Some of the craft were beautifully built yachts up to five or six feet long, and Dad and I spent many interesting sessions watching the racing which took place from time to time.

Kite flying was another popular pastime in the park. I remember one man with a swarthy complexion who wore a tippy cap and spoke with a foreign accent. He looked as if he might have been connected with the sea. He possessed a big box kite, and once in the air it could rise to a great height, possibly up to a thousand feet, and he used a windlass to wind out his reel of thin cord. This huge kite made our conventional children's kites complete with tail look like Lilliputian toys.

On the whole, I think I must have been a reasonably well-behaved child. At any rate, I don't ever remember being on the receiving end of my father's belt. I was in disgrace on one occasion though. On our trips to the town centre, and to see my maternal grandparents near Cannon Street Station, I used to observe how most of the men, when alighting from the tramcar, used

44

to jump off with a deft movement and a slight run before the vehicle stopped. I was most intrigued by this, and to me it stamped them as really masculine, and not like women and children who had to wait until the tram stopped, and then carefully step down.

I determined to have a go at this feat myself, and the opportunity came when we were returning from town, and I was first on to the lower step. As the vehicle was slowing down at the Lee Street stop, I casually stepped off and made a perfect landing, with the customary little run. That was really a proud moment, and I looked round for the appropriate congratulations from my parents. The euphoria faded immediately, though, when I saw the look of horror on my mother's face, and the stern expression on my father's. As we walked down Lee Street, Dad said to me, "Bernie, you shouldn't have done that, it was very naughty, and you might have had a nasty accident. To teach you not to do it again you will go straight to bed without any tea." In vain I protested that I had watched the men do it, and that I knew exactly how to do the little run.

When we got home, upstairs I went, and into bed. While I listened to the rattle of cups and saucers, and the buzz of conversation down below, I reflected that there was little justice in this world. The thing was, I *knew* I could do it properly, and *had* done it. By about 8 o'clock I was feeling really peckish, when to my surprise I heard footsteps coming upstairs and the door opened. It was my mother, bringing me some supper. She didn't say much, just, "You won't do it again, Bernie, will you?" giving me a kiss. Rather shamefacedly, I replied, "No, Mother." And that was the end of that.

At the opposite side of Holderness Road from East Park were a number of short streets named after scientists and engineers, Brindley, Telford, Faraday and Kelvin. Behind them was open ground, fields intersected with ditches, until one came to Southcoates Lane. This rather narrow lane, when it left Holderness Road, curved round almost parallel with the main road, and eventually linked up southward with the main dockland highway, Hedon Road. At its junction with Hedon Road was the forbidding outline of Hull's gaol, surrounded by a high wall with rows of loose bricks on the top. I often wondered what went on behind those gaunt barred windows. Did the inmates spend *all* their time making okum and mailbags? It was many years afterwards before I heard the great doors click behind me as the gaoler doorkeeper turned his key, not, I hasten to add, as a temporary resident, but as a member of a concert party giving a Sunday afternoon programme of entertainment to the prisoners.

At its Holderness Road end, Southcoates Lane was built up for a short distance, ending with Taylor's Laundry. After that, for half a mile or so, it was bordered by open fields and two farm houses, Beadles and Salvidges. Both these farms had big rhubarb beds, and one could buy from either of them an armful of rhubarb, or as much as one could carry, for 2d. Beyond the

45

farms, at an intersection with a new road, Southcoates Avenue, also coming from Holderness Road, a big new building was rising in the autumn of 1911. This was to be Southcoates Lane School, designed to take the overspill from the crowded Estcourt Street and Mersey Street Schools, nearer the city, and also to cater for a new housing estate to the east, which was still only on the drawing board.

I remember going with my parents to have a look at the fine new building, and being told that in a few months' time, it was to be my school. As I have already said, I was never really happy at Mersey Street, and the prospect of being a scholar at this handsome new school gave me a little thrill of anticipation, particularly as one or two of my Lee Street friends were Estcourt Street pupils who like myself would migrate to the centre, and we should be able to travel together. My last term at Mersey Street finished at Christmas 1911, and I must confess that after singing Christmas carols and receiving a gift from the decorated Christmas tree, I felt just a slight nostalgia at leaving for the last time.

Southcoates Lane opened on January 8th, 1912. My sister Dorothy was now fourteen, and had finished her school career at Estcourt Street, while Dennis was not yet two years old, so I was the only one from our family to transfer to the new school on opening day. My mother took me along, and I was introduced, along with several hundred other boys, to the headmaster, Mr. T. E. Mayman. I was just old enough to go into the lowest class in the Senior Boys Department. The Senior Girls, Juniors, and Infants had their own departments in other sections of the complex.

I found myself, along with forty or so others of my age, in the charge of Mr. Butterick. He turned out to be a good teacher, with enough discipline to keep the class in order, but with a friendly manner which made communication easy. It was a delight to have new pens, pencils, rulers, etc., clean, new unspoiled exercise books, and more modern text books. The class rooms were lofty and airy, and as the Senior Boys were on the first floor of our block, those lucky enough to get a desk near the windows had an elevated view for miles over open countryside to the east. Not another building lay between us and the village of Preston except a couple of farmhouses — now there are three housing estates.

From the word "go" Tommy Mayman was determined to make his school the model for the whole city, and so it proved to be. Over the years, pupils from Southcoates Lane gained many scholarships to secondary schools, the ancient Grammar School where Andrew Marvell was educated, and to Hymers College, the local public school. After the first twelve months his desk was seldom without an array of trophies, silver cups, shields, etc., won in the sporting field. In the spring of the year, swallows and house martins regularly nested under the eaves of the school, so it was not to be wondered at that the school's cricket and football teams came to be known as the

"Swallows" and when the blazer badge was designed, the emblem was a swallow on the wing, superimposed on the white rose of Yorkshire.

CHAPTER EIGHT

I have mentioned earlier that my father had a pleasant tenor voice, and did a little photography with his Sanderson stand camera, but an extremely busy working life left him without much time for the arts. He managed, however, a little reading, and was keen on biographies. *The Story of Helen Keller* was a favourite, and another book which interested him was William Booth's *In Darkest England and the Way Out*, a title which probably owed something to Stanley's book on Livingstone, *In Darkest Africa*. Oddly enough he was fond of reading Robert Burns, and I can remember him reciting extracts from *The Cotter's Saturday Night*. His Sanderson camera was an unwieldy looking instrument with enormous bellows, and was used with a tripod. However, it had had little use since coming to Hull.

In the spring of 1912, about the time of the *Titanic* disaster in April, Dad's health began to cause some anxiety. The injury which he had suffered in a fall from the rigging of a ship before his marriage had weakened his kidneys, and he now began to have periodic bouts of sickness and severe headaches. He himself thought these were just symptoms of a chill on the liver, but as his condition did not improve, his doctor arranged for an examination by a consultant. The diagnosis was that Dad was suffering from Bright's Disease, a condition of the kidneys which usually proves fatal as degeneration advances.

There was talk of a move to Brough, and a lighter job as a marine surveyor, but this could only have delayed matters, and Dad determined to carry on as long as possible. The bouts of sickness grew more frequent, and he had to take to his bed from July. From then on until the end came on August 8th, my mother nursed him with all the devotion humanly possible.

My sister Dorothy and I were sitting in the living room, cold with apprehension, when mother came down the stairs and said in a tired voice, "Dad's gone," breaking into a flood of long pent-up tears. Two-year-old Dennis was in bed, and in any case too young to appreciate the tragedy of a promising life ending at the age of 40.

With his Methodist upbringing, Dad had a religious faith which did not desert him as the end drew near. I learned later on, that a day or two before he died, he had told my mother that he had seen the Blessed Saviour standing with outstretched hands on which his name was written, and then with his clear tenor voice he had sung the well-known words, "Before the throne my surety stands, my name is written on His hands."

For me, the next few days proved a traumatic experience. Death and bereavement were things that happened to other people and other families — now the experience was ours. There were lots of comings and goings, and murmured consultations which were not for my ears. The funeral took place on August 11th, but before then I was taken to see my father's body in his coffin upstairs. I was very shocked, but mercifully a little dazed, and not quite able to appreciate the awful finality of the occasion.

The shipyard was closed on the day of the funeral, and as the procession left our house, the hearse was followed by a squad of twelve of Dad's former colleagues and workmates. One of them said later, "We have lost not a master, but a friend." In a strange way, as the coaches drawn by black horses wound their way through the city to the Western Cemetery, it seemed like a triumphal procession and a not unfitting close to a career which had shown much promise, and although not coming to fruition, had left friendship and fragrance in its wake.

Yet during the next few weeks, I felt a great sense of loss, and when I overheard people saying, "Poor Cis" (my mother's pet name), and "Poor children," I felt a burning sense of resentment. At my age, I did not want sympathy, expressed with the best of intentions as it was. Why should it have happened to us? And why had Dad left us to fend for ourselves? Such reasoning was quite illogical, but the experience had been an emotional shock and, after all, I was only eight years of age.

Fortunately, time is a great healer, and gradually these thoughts receded into the background. For one thing, our situation economically was a problem. With the loss on the Sluice Shipyard, Dad had had little chance to save for a rainy day, and all we had in the way of assets was £100 insurance money. Widows' pensions were still a dream for the far-off future, and the only answer for destitute people was "Parish relief." The prospect of having to go cap in hand to the Board of Guardians for a pittance of relief was abhorrent to "respectable" people, so with a little guidance from relatives and friends, we tackled the problem of survival.

What was our potential? My mother, although never robust, was reasonably fit, and prepared to go out to work. My sister Dorothy had left school and was doing a small job of housework, but was capable of better things. This left myself aged eight and Dennis, two. Obviously we could not be left entirely on our own, and the position was met by mother getting a part-time job of office cleaning which meant attendance early and late, but not during school hours.

Dorothy obtained a position in the office of Taylor's Laundry, the proprietor of which, Alderman T. S. Taylor, was a superintendent of Brunswick Wesleyan Sunday School. He knew Dorothy was a bright girl who had paraphrased a sermon and won a book prize which he had offered for the best effort sent in, and she adequately filled a vacancy in the accounts department. So with these sources of income and strict economy in every direction, we managed to keep our heads above water.

Later on, my mother having found office cleaning and running a home much too exacting, another arrangement was successfully tried. This involved Mother taking Dennis to her cousins off Beverley Road, where they

49

had a successful butchery business. Here, her job was to help in the making of brawn, pork pies, etc., for the shop, and to make herself generally useful in the business. This arrangement worked very well for some time, and my mother was much happier working with her relatives. She was also able to keep a watchful eye on Dennis in his pre-school years.

Meanwhile, I was settling down at school, once the shock of bereavement had subsided. From Lee Street, a group of around the same age attended Southcoates Lane Boys' and our route there was usually over the fields mentioned earlier between Holderness Road and Southcoates Lane. These fields were drained by a series of ditches or dykes, some narrow, some quite wide, and they provided us with athletic exercise and some healthy rivalry as we tested our prowess in jumping them.

Some of the bigger boys could cover prodigious distances in their leaps. Approaching with a sprinting run, they would take off with a flying leap and safely negotiate what to us eight- and nine-year-olds seemed almost full-size canals. The biggest ones were no more than three or four feet deep though, and I never heard of any serious accidents.

An incident comes to mind where one of the smaller fry came to grief. I, and one or two boon companions, had successfully jumped one of the smaller ditches, and I am afraid we were convulsed with laughter when Cyril, a year younger than most of us, missed the far bank when jumping, rolled sideways, slid backwards, and ended on his back kicking frantically and yelling, "Mamma! Mamma!" He was in no danger, as the water was only a few inches deep, and he eventually climbed on to the bank covered in green slime, looking a sorry sight as he hurried home instead of continuing to school. We were a heartless lot, and "Mamma's darling" was forbidden to jump ditches any more!

Meanwhile, class work proceeded on its course under Mr. Butterick. I was eager for knowledge — geography, history, and composition being my favourite subjects. I was reasonably good at arithmetic, particularly the mental variety, but when later on we tackled geometry and algebra, I had no enthusiasm for them. In history, I was particularly interested in the period of the Norman Conquest, and the Civil War in which Hull figured prominently. Holding the biggest arsenal outside London, Hull was unsuccessfully besieged by Charles I in 1642 — a stirring chaper in its history. Although realising that Cromwell had the function of Parliament very much at heart, I felt a sneaking regard for the gallant Royalists so faithful to their king.

In geography, we were furnished with brand new school atlases. I took a delight in studying maps, and found them intensely interesting. This trait has remained with me through the years, and I still find great fascination in thumbing through the Oxford World Atlas, and also studying the more specific details of the English and Scottish countryside through the medium of the Ordnance Survey large scape maps.

I don't think I have yet mentioned that I was a natural left-hander, writing and throwing balls with my left hand, using knife and fork the "wrong way round" at home — but not when out to tea! I held a hammer in my left hand when striking nails, kicked naturally with my left foot, and winked with my left eye.

Now, Tommy Mayman, the Southcoates Head, had a thing about handwriting. A flawless writer himself, he insisted that there was only one way to write properly, and he insisted that every pupil used his method. To this end, he would come periodically round the classes and take us for "pen drill" as he called it. On his call of "Pen Drill One!" we placed our right hand wrist down flat on the desk, on "Pen Drill Two!" we placed (with our left hand) the pen firmly, but not too firmly, between first finger and thumb, with the finger slightly curved outward. "Pen Drill Three!" was the signal to bring pen to paper and start writing. Woe betide anyone whose index finger had not got the outward curve! As he wandered among the rows of desks his ruler, or perhaps his cane, would come down "whack!" on the erring joints.

Imagine me, who up to now had always written with the left hand, trying to cope with what to me was an unnatural and crippling position for a pen. However, I survived the frequent raps on the knuckle, and eventually managed to cope with this idea of writing, but never approached the smooth, flowing style of our mentor — or tormentor. Eventually, I lost the desire to use my left hand for writing, and when I left school I had no wish, or even the capability, to write legibly with my left hand. I sometimes wonder what my handwriting would have looked like if I had been allowed to continue left-handed, as of course children naturally "golly-handed" now do, and have done for many years.

Ambidexterity, too, had its drawbacks. Many years later I had a business colleague who could write with either hand at will, and indeed did so, but there was a marked difference in the two styles. On one occasion, following a promotion, he had to submit three specimen signatures for the drawing of cheques. No sooner had these been posted to his head office than he realised that he had forgotten which hand he had used. He had a sleepness night, considering the possibility of cheques being returned with signatures not tallying. Should he own up? If so, what a confession to make at the very outset of his promotion! Eventually, he decided to bank on the probability that he had used his right hand, and to make the point of continuing to use this hand in future. Nothing more was heard of the incident, so either his conjecture was correct, or nobody took any notice of the signatures anyway! The moral is obvious, "Never let thy left hand do what thy right hand should."

At the end of the first school year, in July 1913, when all the routine and end of session exam marks had been totted up, I found to my surprise that I was second in the class — only beaten by Norman, a friend, who also lived in Lee Street. This meant not only that I had won the 2nd Class Prize for the year in standard 3A, but that when we returned after the holidays, Norman and I would have adjacent desks on the back row in the classroom, a prospect which was much to our liking. The book I chose for my prize was *Britain Long Ago*, stories from Old English and Celtic sources retold by E. M. Wilmot-Buxton, a volume that I have read and re-read with interest over the years.

CHAPTER NINE

I had been attending the afternoon class at the Brunswick Wesleyan Sunday School for some time, but to qualify for prizes one had to attend the morning sessions as well. I'm not sure whether it was my mother's suggestion, or my own idea, to try for a prize after seeing the attractive-looking books handed out on prize-giving day, probably a combination of the two. So, at the beginning of January, 1913, I went along to the first morning session of the year, and was duly furnished with a Star Card. These cards, bearing one's name and address, had blanks for each Sunday of the year, and were stamped by the appointed secretary who was supplied with an inked pad and a rubber stamp for the purpose.

The star indicated an attendance, and if one was absent through sickness or holidays, a signed note from a parent resulted in a mark being given. Only those with 100% attendance marks qualified for a prize. The teacher at the afternoon sessions was also a teacher at Southcoates Lane Boys' School. Arthur Stuffins made his lessons interesting, and having become friendly with some of the boys, I had no quarrel with the afternoon attendances.

It was different with the mornings, though, and I could never whip up much interest in the Old Testament stories, which needed special treatment by one with a flair for teaching to be made interesting, and this was not being done at the time. What made matters worse, as far as I was concerned, was that morning scholars, after attending their session, were expected to transfer to the church for the main morning service, which was timed for 10.30. We were marched, supervised by the teachers and the superintendent himself, the Rt. Hon. T. R. Ferens, M.P., from the school building round to the front of the church, and through the main entrance up the wooden stairs into the gallery. There we remained for the whole of the service under the watchful eyes of the great man, T.R.F. himself.

Apart from the children's hymn, and the occasional interesting children's address from the preacher, I found these attendances wearying and boring. There was usually competition to get on to the back row beyond the range of the teaching staff and the superintendent who had his own position in the centre of the serried ranks.

Now and again I managed to make the back row, but it was usually the preserve of the bigger and stronger ones. The woodwork of the pews was amply endorsed with the initials of juvenile occupants, some of the dated ones going back a generation or more. Mine eventually appeared on the hymn book ledge, and presumably were there until the building was demolished to make room for a modern edifice 50 years later.

The forecourt in front of the church had a low coping surmounted with ornamental iron railings, and as we marched from Sunday School to "Chapel" one or two of the more daring boys would sometimes make a dive for a point in the railings where the width between the bars allowed a small body to wriggle through. Then with a triumphant smirk at the rest of us, and the teachers, the successful escapees would be away up the road to the delights of East Park or the playing fields!

I had seen so many successful getaways, that I was determined to have a go when the operation looked likely to succeed. So, one beautiful summer morning, as we filed past the railings, I made a sudden dart and was halfway through when T.R.F., who had spotted the attempt, dashed across and seized the back of my jacket. Pulling me in again, he gave me a shake, saying, "You naughty boy, what do you think you are doing? You will sit with me now." I felt utterly humiliated. Never before had I been in such an ignominious situation. My planned escape to the Elysian Fields had failed completely! Not only was I annoyed with myself for being caught, but the disgrace of being apprehended by the superintendent himself, city benefactor, local M.P. and all, made me cringe with humiliation.

Still grasping me firmly, T.R.F. walked me up the stairs, and I had the doubtful distinction of sitting next to him throughout the service and sharing his bible during the reading of the lessons. He used pince-nez for reading, these spectacles usually danging on a chain when not in use. When he had finished reading, he snickled his nose, and the pince-nez fell off into their usual position. Watching him perform this operation took some of the tedium away from the situation. When the apparently interminable service eventually ended, he said to me, "Well, my boy, I hope this will be a lesson to you. Don't ever try to do such a thing again."

How relieved I was when I was out in the fresh air free again. This incident should have made me dislike T.R.F. for ever. It did for a time, but later on I came to appreciate his many good qualities, his generosity, and his genuine desire to help young people on the somewhat difficult path of moral rectitude, as well as his efforts for them in the realm of physical fitness. His magnificent gifts during his lifetime in the founding of the Hull University, the Ferens Art Gallery, almshouses and playing fields, apart from his business and parliamentary service, make him, without doubt, one of Hull's greatest citizens.

In the meantime, the Sunday School year drew to a close, and I found myself with 100% attendance and qualifying for a prize. The prize distribution day arrived, and I was there with eyes like saucers looking at the pile of delectable appearing books, inside which the secretaries were pasting the labels bearing the names of the recipients. Would mine be a G. A. Henty, or an R. M. Ballantine? Perhaps it would be *Treasure Island* or one of W. H. G. Kingston's, maybe *The Three Midshipmen*.

The euphoria of anticipation came to an end when my name was called, and I went forward to receive my prize. I glanced eagerly at the title. It was *The Last House in London* by Crona Temple, of whom I had never heard.

Stifling my disappointment, I took it home and showed it to my mother. "You'll probably find it quite interesting when you read it," she said. I tried to read it, but alas, I found it the most dreary book I had ever come across, about a widow in a London suburb, quite well-to-do apparently, and her priggish daughter. I never did finish it, and I think it went eventually to a jumble sale.

Curiously enough, I saw the same book in a Hull bookseller's window some time later, and its selling price was 9d. This was the worldly reward for attending Sunday School, morning and afternoon for 52 weeks. Even my mother expressed her surprise and disappointment.

In all fairness, I don't think it was the intention of the Sunday School authorities, least of all T.R.F., that a ten-year-old should be given such a book. I think it was the secretaries, slapping indiscriminately the recipients' labels in the uppermost books on the pile, where the fault lay. However, the morning Sunday School experiment hadn't been a success as far as I was concerned, and in the future, my attendances were confined to the afternoons. On this point, my mother and I were in complete agreement.

She occasionally found time even in this busy period of her life to read a bed-time story to us children, and I always loved these. Favourites for her to dip into, were some bound volumes of *Chatterbox* and *Sunday*. There was ample subject matter, informative as well as fictional in these annuals, most of it interesting and absorbing.

One of the *Chatterboxes* — 1907 I think it was — had a serial story of life at a small residential school in Holderness run by the local rector. It was entitled *His Last Chance*. Although the actual place names were disguised, we were almost certain that "Holmington" was Hornsea, and "Carrswick" where the school was situated, was Garton-in-Holderness. Meetings of the Holderness Hunt came into the story, and there was a graphic account of the wreck of a schooner during a winter storm. Local rivalries also came into the scene. I have sometimes wondered whether Winifred Holtby, whost best-seller *South Riding* became a classic on life in Holderness, ever read this *Chatterbox* story in her youth.

Another book which was popular for bed-time reading was *Talks with the Bairns about Bairns* by Ruth Elliott. The style was typically Victorian, but most of the stories were true ones, and I think my favourites were those of the childhood days of Mozart, and the Scottish naturalist Tam Edward. I still possess this book, which was a Sunday School prize of my father's. Did he attend morning and afternoon for 52 weeks, I wonder? On the fly leaf is written, "Tom Heald — a reward from the Wesleyan Sunday School, South Ferriby, Sept. 1882." Tom, at that time, would be not quite eleven years old. How much more suitable, I have often thought, than the dreary novel which was my Sunday School prize.

Up to now, recreational facilities in East Hull had not been too good.

True, there was East Park, also a paved playground in Dansom Lane, and "Nanny-goat Park," a rectangle of spare ground opposite the Hedon Road Gaol, and which was mainly used for tethering goats and exercising dogs, but was also the venue for scratch games of football played by the local youth. There was, however, need for something more, and with funds supplied by Rt. Hon. T. R. Ferens, of my Sunday School encounter, a boating lake adjacent to the East Park was under construction. Beyond the park, the King George V Playing Fields with cricket and football pitches had just been opened, and here the "Swallows" played their home matches.

Behind the playing fields, on a secluded site, an open bathing pool for boys had been built, with not far away another pool for girls, screened by woodland. Crudely made by modern standards, and with primitive dressing accommodation, they at any rate served the purpose of providing healthy exercise for schoolchildren, and were very popular. At that time, as far as the boys were concerned, there were no regulations regarding the wearing of swimming trunks or slips, and on my first visit, most of the boys were swimming or paddling "au naturel," and obviously enjoying the freedom from restrictive clothing. It all looked very innocent and natural.

In another part of the town a popular place for swimming was the Barmston Drain. Warm water from the Sculcoates Electric Power Station and its cooling system passed into the drain, and "hey presto!" here was a ready-made lido. Boys from the Beverley Road and Northumberland Avenue Schools used it regularly, and swimmers from these two schools used to carry off the prizes at the local swimming galas with great regularity.

Grandma and Granpa Hollingworth lived in a terrace of houses which ended at the drain bank, providing a ready means of access to the "lido" for Northumberland Avenue boys. Here again, nudity was the usual thing, but the arm of the law took a different view, and if a policeman happened to wander down there on his beat, there was a yell of "Copper!" or "Slop!" and little boy "streakers" would be seen sprinting through the terraces to the safety of their homes, clothes in a bundle under their arms. I expect the man on the beat had many a laugh over these proceedings.

CHAPTER TEN

A stone's throw from where we lived was a corner shop kept by two sisters who specialised in home baking, and the Misses E. & B. Belt's cakes, pastries, and home-made bread became very much thought of in the neighbourhood. In December 1913, just before my tenth birthday, they needed an errand boy to deliver their products in the area, and approached my mother to see if she was willing for me to take the job. The income from my sister's work, added to what my mother earned, was only sufficient for us to live extremely modestly.

So any little extra that I could earn was very welcome, and my mother agreed. The job entailed about 1½ hours each day after school, and two hours or so on Saturday mornings. For this, I was paid 9d. per week, which was later increased to 1/-, but I never went home on Friday evening without receiving in addition a pie, or a supply of buns, or scones — "To make me a big boy," they said. They were a good-hearted couple, and Lee Street never seemed quite the same after they retired during the Second World War.

Now I had joined the ranks of the workers! I was supplied with a big rectangular basket which carried about eight two-pound bread loaves wrapped in a white linen cloth, and the occasional bag of pastries or buns. I carried a list of the houses at which to call, and their requirements, and soon got to know the different customers.

After my first fortnight, it was nearly Christmas, and the time for the giving of Christmas boxes to the dustman, milkman, paper boy, etc. "Why not wish your customers a Merry Christmas?" it was suggested at home. "You might get a worth-while response." The idea horrified me and I flatly refused, as it sounded too much like cadging. However, a compromise was reached when my sister later produced a "Compliments of the Season" card which she had seen in a stationer's window, and I was persuaded that showing this to the customers on the couple of days preceding Christmas would produce results.

Rather shamefacedly showing this card I was agreeably surprised at the generosity of most people, and I finished with nearly fifteen shillings, mostly made up of coppers and sixpences. As I was in need of a new pair of boots and fresh underwear, the money was put to good use.

My three years as a baker's errand boy gave me quite an insight into human nature. At some houses my reception was a curt one, and at others just the opposite. One old couple treated me as if I might have been their grandson, and I seldom came away from their house without a sweet, a bar of chocolate, or a copper or two. At several of the bigger houses on Holderness Road, the door was answered by the maid in uniform, and "below stairs" at one of the biggest houses they seemed to have a battery of kitchen and serving maids, usually laughing and joking (and teasing me) until one or other of the various bells rang for attention in another part of the house, when there would be a flurry of activity and adjusting of caps.

After a long session in the darkness of a winter evening I sometimes felt very tired, especially if I faced a long trek home along the main road. If a tradesman's van happened to come along and be going my way, it was a boon and a blessing. Motor traffic was still almost non-existent, and most horse-drawn vans had a step at the rear to enable the driver to open the rear door, and get into the van for his deliveries. It was common custom for boys to cadge a lift by nipping behind the van and sitting on the four or five inches of horizontal step, its upright supporting bar providing a good hand grip.

There was a bakery in East Park Avenue, and their vehicles homeward bound along Holderness Road were a godsend to a tired errand boy. It wasn't long before I picked up the technique of running behind and heaving myself on to the ready-made seat — out of sight of the driver, I should add — as drivers frowned on such practices. If one of them spotted us, the sting of a long whip lash was the penalty, flicked behind at the full extent of his reach.

Sometimes a mean pedestrian would shout to the driver, "Whip behind!" and this was the signal for the whip to come into action. The practice had its dangers: it was possible to unhitch oneself into the path of a following vehicle, but tired, fatigued, and with aching feet, I used to think the ride was worth the risk, and nothing untoward ever happened to me.

Occasionally I used to be sent to a big grocery store at the junction of Prospect Street and Spring Bank. It was one of a row of shops and houses demolished later on when Ferensway was built to provide a direct link between the Beverley Road/Spring Bank corner and Paragon Station. Broadbent's stores had a wholesale as well as a retail business, and I used to go there for cheeses and 7lb. bags of yeast. They were specialists in cheese, and their counter displaying all the different varieties of this commodity was quite a feature.

I always liked these visits, as they meant a ride on the tram to the town centre and back, a much better proposition than trudging the suburban streets. Hull's tram routes were classified by letters, and the appropriate one was displayed in big lettering on the front and rear of the vehicle. Anlaby Road, for instance, was "A," Beverley Road, "B," Holderness Road, "H," and Spring Bank, "S." There were two routes from Holderness Road to the city centre, the direct one via Witham and North Bridge, and a secondary one via Clarence Street and Drypool Bridge through the "Old Town." The latter route's trams bore the letters "T/H" standing for Town/Holderness, and as these trams passed Lowgate corner, they were convenient for East Hull people making for the Corporation Pier and the ferry to New Holland across in Lincolnshire. Alternatively, there was a shortish direct tram route ("P" for Pier) from the City Square, the central terminal for all routes which radiated outward like the spokes of a wheel.

58

Holderness Road, Hull, about 1910. Horse-drawn van is typical of those behind which I used to "borrow" a lift.

59

Hull was plentifully supplied with drapers' stores in the years before the 1914/18 War, all of them locally owned. Hammonds and Thornton-Varleys were there, as were Edwin Davis's and Bladons. Many have since gone, and among these were William Craft & Sons, on Beverley Road, Anstey's at the corner of Charles Street, Waistell's and May-Till-Kirk's in Charlotte Street, and Marris, Willows and Smith, in Whitefriargate. Almost all of these, as far as I recollect, had the curious "overhead railway" method of communication from the counters to a central cashier's office. Money and the bill were placed in a small box on rollers by the counter assistant who pulled a wire which released a spring loaded mechanism, and hey presto, the box glided away on its wires to the cashier. The customer waited a few seconds, and the box glided back with the receipted bill, and any change which was required.

Shop-walkers were the accepted thing in the big stores, important looking people in black jackets and pin-stripe trousers who presumably added tone to the establishment, and recognised well-to-do customers when they drew up in their carriages.

In the arcade between Silver Street and the Market Place, was Marks and Spencer's Penny Bazaar. They sold an amazing variety of articles at what seems the ridiculous price of one penny. Not far away in Whitefriargate was Jackson's (3/9 hats and 10/6 boots) whose sale windows were adorned with life-like drawings of cats advertising their wares. These drawings were the work of Louis Wain who achieved fame as an artist whose portrayal of cats covered every possible mood from sleepy satisfaction to apprehension, astonishment and blind rage.

The Old Town was literally an island. It was the medieval nucleus of the modern city, with the River Hull and the Humber Estuary on two sides, and up to the 18th century a moat in the form of a big arc linking the natural waterways. Behind this moat had been a fortified wall, with a powerful citadel guarding the "Old Harbour" (River Hull) to the east of the river. Entry to the town before its expansion beyond the walls was by three gateways, North Gate near the present North Bridge, Beverley Gate at the entrance to Whitefriargate, and Mytongate between Beverley Gate and the Humber.

These picturesque gateways, the walls and the citadel — which in its heyday was the biggest arsenal outside London — have long ago disappeared to make room for more modern development. It is to be regretted that all these symbols of an historic past were swept away by thoughtless and soulless philistines. Only one tiny fragment escaped the municipal vandalism, and this, a small section of wall with turret, was re-erected in the East Park, the sole remnant of fortressed Kingston-upon-Hull.

With the increase in maritime trade during early Georgian days the Old Harbour became inadequate for the volume of shipping using the port, and in 1778 the first of the "Town Docks" was opened. This was Queen's Dock, entered from the River Hull between North Bridge and Drypool Bridge, and its construction was followed at intervals by Prince's Dock and Humber Dock, all following the line of the old moat. As they were linked with each other, and Humber Dock had a lockpit opening into the Humber estuary, the Old Town remainded surrounded by water.

When the monument to William Wilberforce was erected on the edge of Queen Victoria Square, the bridge crossing the junction of Queen's and Prince's Docks, which reared up to allow the passage of shipping, became known as Monument Bridge. It led to Whitefriargate and the business quarter in High Street. Between 8 and 9 a.m., hundreds of office workers poured over the bridge on their way to work, and not infrequently they were stopped in their tracks to allow ships to pass between the docks. Many a High Street chief clerk has seen the odd member of his staff slink in several minutes late, and said sternly, "Smith, why are you late?" to receive the reply, "Monument Bridge was up, sir." It is said that this stock excuse was offered by latecomers even after the Queen's Dock was filled in, and the bridge was no longer in use! Incidentally, Whitefriargate is never referred to as such by natives of Hull, it always becomes Whitefra'gate.

During my visits to the city, I often walked the short distance to Queen's Dockside to gaze at the shipping, which varied from Humber sailing keels and sloops, to schooners with their tall rigging, and coasters from English and the near continental ports. Overall, there was a scent of tarry rope and fresh paint which over sixty years later I recall with nostalgia. Fussy little tugs would sometimes draw a string a barges from dock to dock. Occasionally a capstan would be used to move a ship from one berth to another, and my mother recalled as a child hearing the sailors singing shanties as the big capstan wheel was hauled round by manpower, but the picturesque habit of singing shanties had gone in my time with the introduction of steam capstans.

The big ocean-going ships sailing to faraway ports occupied berths in Alexandra Dock to the east of the city. The story of this dock is the saga of a brave local enterprise which deserved to succeed, and nearly did. In the 1880's a consortium of local businessmen, disturbed by the monopoly of transport which the North Eastern Railway had in the city and port, and ignoring its potential, as they thought, in favour of Tyneside, determined to have a railway built linking Hull with the Midland Railway and its ramifications, at Barnsley.

Associated with this idea was a scheme to build a modern dock to attract bigger ships to the port, the dock to have the benefit of this new railway link. So the Hull and Barnsley Railway Company was floated with capital raised in the money market. The railway scheme envisaged bridging the River Ouse near Drax and continuing eastward via Howden and the Caves to the natural barrier of the Wolds which it approached via Drewton Dale. Here, a mile long tunnel through the solid chalk was planned, the line then to continue via Willerby and Springhead to an eastern passenger terminus in George Street. A commercial spur was to run from Sculcoates to the new dock on Hedon Road to be known as the Alexandra Dock in honour of the Princess of Wales as she was at that time, later on the consort of King Edward VII.

One excellent feature of the scheme was that the line was planned to be a high level one, the embankment employed thus cutting out the necessity for level crossings, with which the North Eastern was plagued as mentioned earlier. The North Eastern in its Hull section crossed every main road into the city (except Hedon Road) via a level crossing. True, when it was built in the 1840's, most of the lines were beyond the built-up area, but little foresight was shown for the rapid development of the city, and these level crossings were a perpetual source of irritation to road users for many years. In the twenty-four hours of the day, I believe the Anlaby Road crossing on the main artery of the city was opened and closed not far short of a hundred times.

Unfortunately for the Hull and Barnsley directors and shareholders, the amount of capital raised was not sufficient to see the whole scheme through. The line and the dock were built, my grandfather Hollingworth being one of the army of men engaged in the construction of the latter. But the scheme for a city terminal passenger station in George Street had to be abandoned, and instead the line terminated as I indicated in an earlier chapter, in the inconvenient backwater of Cannon Street with unworthy facilities for its patrons.

Passenger-wise, the Hull and Barnsley Railway was never able to compete with the North Eastern, whose fast services to Leeds via Selby and London via Doncaster were never really at risk. It did, however, attract a good deal of commuter business from Willerby, Kirkella, and South Cave into Hull, and its route through the Wolds, pretty by any standard, was later on, when rambling became popular, a favourite stepping off area for walkers. One outing which many years later my family and I frequently enjoyed was to take the train to Little Weighton, walk over the high wolds below which the line burrowed, and drop down into Drewton Dale via Weedley Springs where one could find a choice of secluded picnicking places. At Weedley Springs a flow of deliciously cool clear water welled from the chalk, providing a refreshing drink on a hot day. After a leisurely walk to South Cave station, the H. & B. provided a quick return to the city.

Between the wars, when the big grouping of the railways came about, and the London and North Eastern came into being, a link was made between the Hull and Barnsley and North Eastern lines so that H. & B. passenger trains were able to run into Paragon Station, and Cannon Street fell into disuse. Then a few years after the Second World War the Hull and Barnsley line was closed, apart from its dock branch, and a brave scheme came to an end.

However, the dock part of the organisation was a success from the start, and Alexandra Dock played a major role in the development of the port. A good deal larger than any of the Town Docks, it had berths for the bigger ocean-going vessels, and with its massive coal hoists, a thriving trade in coal exporting from the South Yorkshire pits was soon on the way, and the high level line carrying long trains of coal wagons without the necessity of level crossings, proved a great boon.

I referred earlier in this chapter to the Wilberforce Monument then standing in the Queen Victoria Square, and since removed to Queen's Gardens, so a word or two about William Wilberforce might not be out of place here.

Born in High Street, Hull, in 1759, he represented Yorkshire in Parliament for many years, and devoted most of his life to campaigning for the abolition of slavery. He turned his back on high political office, and it is said that he could even have had the premiership when Pitt the Younger died, had he so wished. Success in his campaign came in 1833 when the bill to free all slaves in the British Empire finally came before Parliament, and was passed. Wilberforce, who died that year, had the great joy of knowing that his life's work had succeeded.

Wilberforce House in High Street, now a museum of the slave trade as mentioned in the first chapter, should not be missed by visitors. It may not be generally known that the great man had a charming and witty sister who was of much help to him in his early election campaigns. On one occasion when she rose to speak, the crowd cheered and chanted, "Miss Wilberforce for ever! Miss Wilberforce for ever!" When the noise subsided she smiled at them and said, "Thank you all very much for your greeting, but really, you know, I don't wish to remain Miss Wilberforce for ever."

Queen Victoria Square has associations with another prominent son of Hull in the shape of John Bacchus Dykes, composer and musician, who was born in the town where his father was a banker, in 1823 and died in 1876.

The grandfather of J. B. Dykes was incumbent of St. John's Church when Dykes was a boy. This church, at the time of which I am writing, stood on the site of the present Ferens Art Gallery. It became redundant owing to the near proximity of the parish church of Holy Trinity, and was demolished as I well remember in the nineteen twenties.

Young Dykes, a musician to his finger tips, learned to play the piano and violin at a very early age, and at the age of ten he was playing the organ at St. John's, when his feet would hardly reach the pedals. It is recorded that his two sisters were paid a halfpenny per hour for acting as organ blowers during this period! In addition to his talents as a musician, young John had a nice treble voice, and a good story is told of one of his exploits in this field. It was in

1834, when he was eleven, that an important musical festival was being held in Holy Trinity Church. Knowing how well he could sing and read music, the lady sopranos smuggled him into their midst in the chorus.

However, the keen-eyed conductor and adjudicator, Sir George Smart, spotted the lad and had him smartly ejected, much to his chagrin and the disappointment of the ladies! They little knew what a future music maker they had in their midst, a Yorkshireman who gave the world such splendid hymn tunes as *Gerontius* (Praise to the Holiest in the height), *Hollingside* (Jesu, Lover of my soul), and *Melita* (Eternal Father, strong to save).

CHAPTER ELEVEN

The spring of 1914 arrived with little indication to most people of the cataclysm not far ahead, although we heard gossip that the German army was building up, and the Royal Navy was increasing its size and fire power. Anyway, the Triple Entente between Britain, France and Russia was surely an insurance against any trouble in Europe.

Domestic life in East Hull went on as it had done. Apart from my errand boy's job, I had tasks to do in the home. These included chopping firewood for "kindling" and cleaning the downstairs windows. My mother cleaned the upstairs ones, and as they were of the sash type she used to sit on the windowsill with legs inside the bedroom, pulling the upper panes down until she could reach them with the washleather. I sometimes wondered what would happen if she lost her balance, but she never did.

The job I disliked most was cleaning the knives, forks and spoons. This was before the days of stainless steel and had to be done every Saturday, by which time the cutlery was pretty well tarnished. The cleaning was done by rubbing with metal polish on a cloth, usually Silvo, which with Brasso was a product of Reckitts factory in Dansom Lane. Then the metal polish had to be rubbed off with another cloth, and all the cutlery finished off by polishing with a clean duster.

Sometimes mother would take pity on my fumbling away with the metal polish, and would do this part of the operation herself, leaving me to do the cleaning off and final polishing. Now and again she would examine the prongs of the forks which I had finished, to see if any of the Silvo had been left between the prongs. Rejects had to be finished off properly! With Dorothy out at work and Dennis still only four years old, I was the obvious one to do some of the household chores.

I still had time for street games, though. In Lee Street we had a varied repertoire of team games most of which have probably faded into oblivion. "Relievo" was a popular one in which one team had to capture members of the opposing team one by one and they were then "imprisoned" until "relieved" or set free by one of his comrades penetrating the prison territory in a determined dash and shouting "Relievo!" while the defenders with rugby tackles endeavoured to stop him. An advantage of this game was that any number of players could participate provided that there were equal numbers on both sides. When all the imprisoned team had been relieved the roles were reversed, and attackers became defenders. As this game sometimes resulted in torn jackets or trousers it wasn't too popular as far as parents were concerned, and a leisurely version called "Block" which operated without tackling and required more finesse was sometimes played.

Another one was "Three men come seeking work" and this was for six players, three on each side. We would toss for first turn in what was a kind of

65

acting charade. The team winning the toss would go to the opposite side of the street and after a consultation select their trade, or form of employment. It might for instance be "felling timber" or "laying drainpipes." Let's say it was the former. The three would then cross the street to their opponents, and their captain would say "F.G.-T.F.," the first and last letters of the occupation, and the three would then proceed to act the work. Their opponents had to guess the occupation — a wrong guess was replied to with a shake of the head. But if one of them called out "Felling Timber!" the other three had to turn round and dash back across the street before one of the guessing team was able to tap any one of them on the shoulder or back. If they succeeded in this, the roles were reversed, the teams changing sides, but if not, the guessing team had to try again with a different occupation. One of the secrets of success was to think of some outlandish occupation which still had credulity, but would baffle one's opponents. I have wondered since if the television panel game of "What's My Line?," which had such a run of popularity, had its origins in this pastime of ours.

A perennial favourite was "Egg if you move." This was a ball game with only one team involved, and a selected member would thrown the ball in the air — or against a wall — calling out the name of one of the others. The caller, with the rest of the team, had to run as far as possible from the site while the called one had to catch the ball as quickly as possible, and as soon as he had done so, shout out "Egg if you move!" The others then had to stop immediately, or become "Eggie," i.e. the one to throw the ball. If they all stopped on the call, the player with the ball aimed at the nearest, and if the ball touched him he was "it." If not, they all gathered together again, the ball was thrown up and he had to try again. There was a variation of the game where the person whose name was called had the right to claim "three strides and a spit" in the direction of the one he had chosen to aim at — not very hygienic, but usually effective! The streets being virtually traffic free, apart from the occasional horse-drawn rully, these games could be played in safety, whereas today they would be highly dangerous if not impossible.

A game which could only be played in the dark was "Monkeys in the wood." In this, a home base was decided upon, usually a passage between two houses, or a terrace end, and one of the number was allowed to disappear into the darkness beyond the range of the vision supplied by the gas lamps. When he was at a safe distance he would call "Monkeys in the wood!" and the others set off to catch him. The call was continued at intervals, and the object of the hunted one was to dodge the searchers and arrive back at base without being detected. This was aided by ingenuity displayed in dodging down passageways or behind bushes in gardens. Occasionally one would surprise, as I remember doing, a pair of lovers having a kiss and a cuddle in one of the dark passages, and be unceremoniously told where to go!

At the previous Christmas, with some gift money, I had bought a little paraffin hand lamp complete with wick and a container for the oil. It had a revolving top which, when turned round, shut off the light, and it became a dark lantern, similar in fact to those the police used in the days before electric torches, but smaller. As can be imagined, this lantern was in great demand when playing "Monkeys in the wood."

Marbles, of course, were always popular, and the games were usually played with "glass-oggs," the round stoppers from lemonade bottles. These games were played in two ways, either by extracting a piece of macadam from the roadway and using the hole for sinking the marble, or as an alternative moving along the gutter between the "flags" — or pavement — and the roadway, working the marbles along in a kind of continuous game of bowls.

The gas lamp standards, besides being a recognised rendezvous, were useful as substitute stumps when playing street cricket, but this practice was frowned upon by nearby inhabitants whose windows were at risk when boundary hitters, or budding Jessops, were at the wicket. The lamp standards were popular from another angle. We used to vie with each other in seeing who could swarm up the standards in the quickest time, and perch on the horizontal arms at the top, which were provided to rest the ladders of workmen who cleaned the glass faces or repaired the lamps. I happened to be one of the quicker climbers, and we used to jeer at the ineffectual attempts of those boys who hadn't a clue as to how to grip the standard with their legs and swarm up like latter-day monkeys. Another use for lamp standards was as make-shift maypoles. With the aid of a length of rope slung over the horizontal arms, one could indulge in an exhilarating swing as the rope coiled itself round the standard.

Hooliganism, apart from schoolboy pranks, as I remember those days, was practically non-existent. There was the occasional broken window if a ball was mis-directed, and if this happened, the culprit usually owned up and offered to pay for the damage, but wanton destruction was almost unheard of. We sometimes rang door bells and ran away before the householder answered the door, but one soon tired of this prank.

There was one bell, however, which really invited the full treatment. It was at the vicarage which stood at the junction of Lee Street with Holderness Road. As one passed along the pavement, the bell-push was within easy reach of any passer-by as it was only just behind the border fence, and was a source of great temptation to small boys — Satan in the guise of a bell-push, *and* at the vicarage! Eventually, the maid got tired of answering the door and a protective cowl was installed which effectively put an end to the practice.

The vicarage at that time had a very long garden, some of which was later sold for a building site, but in those days the garden ended with a shrubbery, or copse, full of hazels and elders. On one occasion, two of the Williams boys, who lived near us, and myself were anxious to obtain suitable saplings for

67

making bows and arrows. The vicarage copse was the obvious answer. It was bounded by a fairly high wooden fence which we thought we could negotiate without too much difficulty, so we waited one day until the coast was clear, and swarmed over.

Harry was twelve, his brother Reggie was nine, and I was ten, and Harry possessed a clasp knife. Once over the fence we looked towards the french windows of the vicarage, perhaps eighty yards away, and as no-one was in sight, we selected a nice-looking hazel. Harry with his clasp knife was soon at work hacking branches off which would be just the job for our purpose, when the french windows burst open, there was a shout, and the vicar himself was hurtling in our direction. We all made a dash for the fence, and Harry and I managed to scramble over, but Reggie's foot slipped and, before he could recover, the vicar bore down on him and grasped his jacket. Harry and I made ourselves scarce, leaving Reggie to face the music. We felt very crestfallen and shamefaced about this, and hung around in the distance until about ten minutes later Reggie appeared, rather subdued. The vicar had given him a lecture on the sanctity of private property, and extracted a promise not to enter the vicarage grounds on such an errand again.

Boys can be heartless at times — or thoughtless. One of our number in Lee Street was learning to play the piano, and after school had to complete half an hour's practice before being allowed out to play. Sometimes we would stand outside his house and from the pavement peer into the front room — there was a foot or two of garden, with railings, between the pavement and the window, fortunately. Now and again he would turn his head and see us grinning at him, or making faces. This used to make him furious, and if he had gone out of the room to tell his parents he would have had us to face the next day with calls of "tell-tale!" so he took it out of the piano by banging on the keys, after giving us a scowl. He had the last laugh, though, for later on be became quite an accomplished pianist.

The big event in the late spring of 1914 was the visit in June of King George V and Queen Mary to open the new dock. I mentioned earlier how I had been taken by my father three years previously to see the preliminary excavations, and now it was ready for the opening ceremony. With its water area of 53 acres, its entrance lock 750 feet long and 85 feet wide, it was the biggest dock on the East Coast, outside London.

The opening day saw June at its best, sunny and warm, and elaborate preparation had been made for the Royal visit. The route from the Guildhall along Hedon Road to Marfleet was gay with bunting. Parties of school children had been allocated sites on the route, standing on staging so that they could get a better view. I was among the children from Southcoates Lane School, and we were allotted a position just beyond the Gaol, midway long the route. Complete with Union Jacks we gathered at the school and marched to the scene to take up our places. Every few yards lining the roadway was a guardsman standing at ease, in full dress scarlet uniform. On this section they were Coldstreamers, and as I was positioned just behind one of them I was able to take in every detail of his resplendant uniform.

After what seemed an interminable waiting time, there was a murmur, "They're coming! They're coming!" and there in the distance we could see a line of horse-drawn open carriages approaching. An officer near us shouted "Present Arms!" and the soldiers sprang to the command, then stood like statues. There was a tumult of cheering, we all waved our Union Jacks, shouting "Hip! Hip! Hurray!" and the King, looking rather grave, raised his arm in our direction. The Queen, looking every bit her regal self as we had seen her in pictures, wore a slight smile. It was a thrilling moment. Here in the flesh were the two figures who had become so familiar to us in illustrations on chocolate boxes and porcelain articles of every description. Such a brief scanning, and they were past, and it was somebody else's turn to gaze in awe and wonder at the symbols of the British Empire at its might.

With the usual ceremony the new dock was declared open, and from then on it was to be known no longer as "Joint Dock" but as the "King George V Dock." A feature of the dockland area was the huge grain silo specially built for the imports of wheat from Canada via Montreal and the St. Lawrence River, and the United States. Joseph Rank and Sons, the millers, had their headquarters in Hull, the Clarence Street Mills near Drypool Bridge being the biggest industrial premises in the port. Joseph Rank was a native of Hull, and his original windmill was situated on Holderness Road not half a mile from where we lived. Its milling days were long since over, and at that time it was used as a warehouse but still retained some character even without its sails.

CHAPTER TWELVE

In 1914 Hull was well off for entertainment. Its two principal theatres were the Grand and the Alexandra in George Street and Charlotte Street respectively. The "Alex" had a high tower at the top of which a searchlight had been installed, and after dusk in the autumn and winter seasons its light used to pierce the darkness as it swept round the compass like the rays from a lighthouse. These two theatres received visits from London companies touring the provinces, and I seem to remember seeing the advertising bills for *A Royal Divorce* which was touring the country about that time. The Carl Rosa Opera Company paid regular visits, and in my ignorance of grand opera at ten years of age I thought that *Carmen* had something to do with tram drivers and conductors.

The Tivoli and Palace on Anlaby Road were popular variety theatres, and George Robey was always an attraction. A very old music hall, the Empire, stood at the corner of George Street and Grimston Street, but was about to be pulled down to make way for a new cinema, the Majestic. Hull's first cinemas were the Kinema-Color in Carr Lane, and the Prince's Hall in George Street, both opened in 1910. I remember being taken to the Prince's in its early days and watching the antics of the Keystone Cops, to the accompaniment of suitable music on the piano. Later on came Charlie Chaplin in such films as *Charlie in the Park*. In the novely value of motion pictures the strutting figures and flickering screen were accepted without question.

In our family circumstances, visits to the cinema were few and far between, but by 1914 cinemas were springing up in various parts of the city, and a big one in East Hull was the Holderness Hall at the junction of Holderness Road and Witham. The weekly programme published in advance was used as a sales gimmick by the proprietors who arranged for certain deliberate mistakes to be incorporated in the printing. Patrons were invited to spot the mistakes and underline them, giving the correct spelling, and to post or deliver the entry in an envelope with name and addressd included. The first three correct entries opened early on Monday received two tickets for the best seats in the balcony.

Harry and Reggie Williams, of the unfortunate vicarage episode, had been to the Holderness a few times and had attempted the competition without success. It was Harry who hit on an idea worthy of Sherlock Holmes. If it was the first three correct entries opened on the Monday morning which gained the free tickets, then these must have been taken from the top of the pile. It followed that the later the entries were delivered, the better the chances were of being opened first. He suggested that we three put our heads together and form a little syndicate with a view to spotting the errors, and taking turns to put the envelope containing the entry through the cinema letter box late on Sunday evening.

The Williams boys had a "den" in their garden — a little wooden hut — where we arranged to meet and search for the mistakes. As Harry was the instigator (and the eldest!) it was agreed that the first entry should be his, and it was duly taken along to the cinema. Imagine our delight when that week's results were published in a later programme, to find that he was one of the winners! He and I went along one convenient evening, it having been agreed that Reggie should have the next turn, and we felt rather like royalty as we walked up the thickly carpeted stairs and were ushered into the front row of the balcony. I can't remember what the main film was, but I think it may have been one of the *Exploits of Elaine*. Lolling back in those comfortable seats with no need to crane one's neck as in the pit stalls, and spending a penny on an ice cream in the interval, was indeed ecstasy.

Reggie had his turn later, for the idea succeeded on several occasions over the next few months. Whether the management "rumbled" us or not, we never knew, but later on they dropped the idea, and our brief spell of membership of the affluent society was over.

The months before the outbreak of the First World War were relatively care-free ones for most people. Those were the days when well-dressed young men appeared in spats, lemon coloured gloves, and bowlers or straw hats, swinging a walking stick. Popular songs of the time were *Molly Morgan, Hello, Hello, Who's you lady friend?*, and *Who were you with last night?* Comic picture postcards were very subdued and chaste compared with later years. I remember one being sent to us which caught my eye. It showed the rear view of two men walking along, one of them wearing a norfolk jacket and knee breeches. He had his hands in his breeches pockets, this pushing up the back of his jacket. Walking behind him was his small daughter, copying his stance with back of frock pushed up showing an expanse of frilly knickers, and hands where pockets would have been in male attire. The caption was "Following in Father's Footsteps."

Boys' periodicals and comics were plentiful. *Comic Cuts* detailed the adventures of Dreamy Dan and Tired Tim, while *Gem, Magnet* and *Boys' Friend* were extremely popular, and most third and fourth formers avidly awaited the latest adventures of Tom Merry, Arthur Augustus D'Arcy, Billy Bunter, and Jimmy Silver, emanating from the fertile imagination of Frank Richards during many decades. Another favourite boys' weekly was *Chums*. I could not afford a regular periodical, but some of these mentioned were passed around among my friends, and about this time I was given by the Williams family a number of the monthly issues of the *Boys's Own Paper* for 1890 and 1891 — it must have been spring cleaning time! I also received some copies of the B.O.P. for 1911-12 from Harold Watson mentioned earlier.

The contrast between the Victorian and the more recent issues of the B.O.P. was quite remarkable, both in layout and contents. Illustrations in

71

the earlier ones were mostly line drawings and rather crudely processed photographs, while in the later ones lots of colour pictures appeared, and the printing was much bigger and easier on the eyes. These were the days when such cricketing giants as Jack Hobbs, C. B. Fry, Herbert Strudwick, and the famous pair of Yorkshiremen, George Hirst and Wilfred Rhodes, were in their prime. I revelled in the accounts of their exploits against the Australians in the shape of Victor Trumper, Warren Bardsley and C. G. Macartney.

Another children's periodical which deserves mention was the *St. George's Magazine*, a monthly, and very popular in the education world. Its sales were fostered at some of the schools, and my sister Dorothy used to get copies when she attended Estcourt Street School. If *St. George's* had a slight educational slant, its contents were very readable, and its nature articles were lively and interesting. All these periodicals and magazines have passed into oblivion, and nothing as good seems to have taken their place — certainly not the horrendous cartoon types of "comics" on sale to latter-day juveniles.

In the 1913-14 school year I was in Arthur Stuffins IVA class, and it was an agreeable time. I mentioned earlier that I was also in his Sunday afternoon class at the Brunswick Wesleyan Chapel at that time, as were one or two others including Clarence Bratley and Jim Butters, both bright youths, who had recently been transferred to Southcoates Lane from Craven Street on a re-distribution arrangement. Jim and I became good friends, and over sixty years later still corresponded although half a world separated us as he was domiciled in Australia until he died recently. Schoolboy dress at this period usually consisted of eton collar, jersey, and short trousers. Knickerbockers had gone out and the bare knees era was just in the future, for our "short" trousers were of knee length. The eton collars purchased by my mother were made of linen, and frequent washing was necessary — and ironing. Celluloid collars were worn by some boys, but these were inflammable and highly dangerous if in the proximity of a naked flame, as Jim Butters had found out some time previously when his celluloid collar had erupted into flame in a home accident, and badly burned his neck. I believe that, later on, celluloid collars were banned from sale by law.

It was a custom of Tommy Mayman, the headmaster, to look in at the various classes from time to time to see how things were going. His rulings on handwriting have already been mentioned. On one occasion, he came in when we were studying poetry from an educational anthology, and had the bright idea of seeing how much we knew by heart. "Now, boys," he said, "I'm going to read a passage, and when I stop I want you to follow on with the next verse, in turn." Then he started quoting from such poems as Wordsworth's *Daffodils*, Cowper's *Loss of the Royal George* and *Alexander Selkirk*, and Shelley's *The Cloud*. If a boy couldn't continue, he dropped out and the next one took over — it was a kind of elimination game.

One after another dropped out, until there were only three of us left,

72

Clarence, another boy and myself. Dipping as he did at random from the book we followed on with every quotation he threw at us, until at last he closed the book. "Well done, lads," he said. "That was really excellent. You deserve something for such first class knowledge and memory." Then he pulled some change from his trousers pocket, and shouting "Catch!" threw us each a shilling. Then he murmured something to Arthur Stuffins, who presumably had been wondering how it would all end, and walked out to his next assignment. This incident was typical of the man — he would come down heavily on scroungers, but was always ready to encourage diligence and industry.

One of the features at Southcoates Lane was the periodic observance of fire drills. We would be absorbed in an essay or an arithmetical problem, when suddenly we would hear Tommy Mayman's whistle giving six short blasts. Immediately we downed tools, put books in desk, and at the double were out of the classroom and down the nearest flight of stone stairs to assemble in orderly fashion in the school playground where Tommy was standing, watch in hand. When the last pupil and teacher were out, he would look at his watch and say, "Very good, we've knocked ten seconds off the previous record." Then we dismissed, and returned to our classrooms at a much more leisurely gait.

Tommy Mayman, in addition to being a first class headmaster and disciplinarian, had also the common touch, and pupils or parents could approach him with confidence if they had problems. In his first two-and-a-half years at Southcoates Lane up to the summer of 1914, he had fostered such a spirit of "esprit de corps" that every boy was proud to be one of the "Swallows" of Southcoates Lane School. His football team had already won the Firbank Shield and the Hull Schools Cup, the former for topping the Schools' League, and the latter for winning the knock-out competition, and these two trophies graced his desk in the hall.

He was a member of the Hull Bicycle Club, and used to come to school from time to time on his Dursley-Pedersen machine, with its cantilever frame, wide range 3-speed gear, and hammock saddle. This unusual if not revolutionary bicycle had quite a vogue among cycling connoisseurs in the first two decades of the century, and it and the Golden Sunbeam were looked upon as the aristocrats of the pedalling world, at any rate where the pastime of cycle touring was concerned.

He was also a lover of classical music and an accomplished flautist. It was his practice to end the school year with a concert, and the July 1914 event was a memorable one. 1914 really was the end of an epoch, for when we returned to school in late August, World War One had started — but more of that later. Those of us who kept up with the news knew that Archduke Francis Ferdinand, heir to the Austrian throne, had been assassinated on

Serbian soil on 28th June, but had little thought of its impending significance for Europe and the world.

Additional to the musical items at the concert, one of which was a turn on the piccolo by a youngster of Russian descent named Kostrovitsky (who later became a valued member of the Hull Philharmonic Society), was a recitation by another pupil, Andy Wilson, of *Play the Game* by Sir Henry Newbolt. Kiplingesque as it was, and redolent of Britain at the height of her colonial power, I have never forgotten Andy's rendering, with its "The Gatling's jammed and the colonel dead, and the regiment blind with dust and smoke," through to "But the voice of a schoolboy rallied the ranks — Play up! Play up! and play the game."

Andy was about a year older than I was, and he and his younger brother John were the sons of Mr. Jack Wilson, for many years the secretary of the Northern (Rugby) Union, which later became the Rugby League.

Andy, a big raw-boned blonde, soon afterwards went on from Southcoates Lane to the Hull Technical College. Later, as a keen cyclist, he joined the Hull Thursday Road Club which produced many fine racing cyclists, but none so good as Andy. In his brief racing career as a time-trialist, he held nearly every national record, including, I believe, the York-London, and London-Edinburgh records.

At the height of his racing career he caught a heavy chill which turned to pneumonia, and to the great sorrow of all who knew him, he died at the early age of 23. In his memory, the Hull Thursday Road Club organised an annual competition for the "Andy Wilson Memorial Trophy," one of the wheels of Andy's racing cycle, and this trophy is competed for in perpetuity.

The school year ended on a satisfactory note as far as I was concerned, when to my considerable surprise Arthur Stuffins told me that I had come top of the class in arithmetic, and consequently qualified for the IVA Arithmetic prize. I knew my marks had been consistently good, but not, I had thought, so good as to win a special prize. When the time came to choose a book — we had some choice in titles — I had no hesitation in choosing W. H. G. Kingston's *The Three Midshipmen*, in the Everyman's de-luxe edition. This was a great book for boys, and I later revelled in the advantures of Jack Rogers, Alick Murray and Terence Adair around the oceans of the world.

So we broke up for the holidays, and in the intervals between household chores and my bread delivery round, I found time for games with the Williams boys either in Lee Street or the park. The Williams were a large family, and in addition to Harry and Reggie already mentioned, were Eddie the eldest, Kathleen, Stanley, and two younger ones, Denis and the baby, Rene. Denis, spelt with one "n," was the same age as my brother Dennis, now four years old, and these two became great friends. I have sometimes heard them described as the "Heavenly Twins" but oftener than not "The Terrible Twins." The older Williams boys were pioneer members of the 1st

74

Holderness Sea Scouts, of which their father was scoutmaster, and very smart they looked in the navy type caps, neckerchieves, blouse and shorts.

Baden-Powell, when he started the Boy Scout movement in 1908, had included the somewhat revolutionary shorts and bare knees in the uniform, and this style was now very slowly beginning to catch on for everyday use. For "Sunday" wear, the usual dress for the 10-14 age group was a Norfolk jacket with knickerbockers buttoned below the knee. Caps were normally worn — it was most unusual to see any young males bare-headed, and as we grew older we sported for week-end wear in the summer time, a boater, or, as we used to call them, "straw benjies" which later became "straw bangers."

CHAPTER THIRTEEN

My mother had arranged for me to spend a fortnight of my holidays with Grandma Heald in her cottage at South Ferriby, so the last week of July saw me on the *Isle of Axholme* (which had now replaced the old *Her Majesty*) bound for Ferriby Sluice. The hour's cruise up the Humber was full of interest as usual, with noisy black-headed and common gulls following the vessel astern. We passed close in to St. Andrew's Dock with its fleet of trawlers, and a group of naked boys bathing or sitting in the sun on the retaining wall waved to us as we passed by. On our left beam we saw New Holland Pier and one of the white-funnelled G.C.E. ferry boats moored there.

Then the chalk walls of "Little Switzerland" appeared through the trees at Hesslewood, before we turned across the river towards the Lincolnshire side to avoid Redcliff Sand, one of the many shoals which are a menace to Humber shipping at low water. Then we had a look at Barton Waterside and the chalk gash of Ferriby Cliff before we turned into the narrows between Read's Island and the Lincolnshire bank with its white-pebbled beach, known to the local inhabitants as "checkers."

I could see Uncle Joe's house at the edge of the Wold escarpment, before sighting our old house, "Oakdene," and Sluice Mill, as we turned into Ferriby Sluice Haven. As we gently kissed the jetty, with Captain Maltby's usual precision, the engine room telegraph clanged "Stop Engines." The gangway was run out, passengers streamed ashore, and another Humber crossing was over.

I sought out Mr. Melton, the bearded Ferriby carrier — or he sought me out — and I rode with him on the carrier's cart up the mile long road from Sluice Haven to South Ferriby. Grandma had a delicious meal waiting, with brawn and cold meat and home-made cakes, and I was ready for a fortnight's bliss.

The next morning Uncle Joe called round, and after greeting Grandma, said to me, "Now Bernie, how would you like to come with me as far as Elsham tomorrow? I shall be delivering that way." I didn't need twice asking, for the chance of a ride in the horse and cart through the villages was too good to be missed. "Right," said Uncle Joe, "I'll be round about nine-thirty." So, on a beautiful July morning, I climbed up beside him, and we set off along the Horkstow road.

The wayside villages between the Wolds and the Ancholme valley stretched like a string of pearls between South Ferriby and Brigg — Horkstow, Saxby, Bonby, Worlaby, Elsham — they all had something of interest, but perhaps the prettiest was Saxby, or to give it its full title, Saxby-All Saints. On this hot morning Saxby village with its ancient church almost hidden among the trees looked deliciously cool and inviting. A call with a joint of sirloin at Mrs. Goodwin's, with a bit of good-natured banter exchanged at most houses, enlivened the journey.

There was just one incident when I almost panicked. It was while visiting a house at Worlaby where a small business matter had to be discussed, that my uncle was away rather a long time. In the heat, the horse began to get restive, and I wondered however much longer I should have to be in sole charge. It pawed the ground impatiently, then waggled its ears and shook its head as irritating flies buzzed around its face. Finally, champing at the bit and with a kick of the legs, it decided to set off. Feeling quite terrified, I hung on to the reins and shouted without much effect, but fortunately my uncle had heard the shouts, and dashing out of the house, sprinted alongside and seized hold of the reins near the horse's head as it was about to get into a gallop, and gradually pulled it to a standstill. A quiet reprimand to the horse, and a pat or two on the flanks followed, while the animal recovered its composure, and after a brief pause we were on our way again.

"Were you frightened, Bernie?" Uncle Joe asked. "Well, yes, I was," I answered. "I was wondering what would happen if he really got away, then you came out." "I shouldn't have been so long," he said, "But when a horse gets restless, the best thing to do is to stand by its head, holding the reins tightly. Anyway, I hope it doesn't happen again." It didn't, but I felt rather subdued for the rest of the trip, and was relieved when we arrived back in Ferriby again. I picked up considerably, though, when Uncle Joe remarked as I climbed out of the seat, "I shall be going to Winterton on Friday in the car, how about coming with me then?" "Oh, yes, please," I answered, "I should like that very much." "Right-o," he said, "I shall be round at Grandma's about two o'clock."

Now, Uncle Joe had recently become the possessor of a Model T Ford car, one of the few cars in the village, and as I had never ridden in a motor car before, I was thrilled at the prospect. The next day or two seemed to pass so slowly, but I did a few errands, and visited my father's cousins, the Andrews. Frank, one of the Andrew brothers, kept the village stores, on the High Street, known locally as "Top" Street, and when I called in with an order from Grandma, he usually gave me a stick of Devonian toffee, or some other confectionery.

Friday eventually arrived, and soon after two o'clock there was a hoot outside the front door, and the noise of a panting engine. I quickly opened the door, and to Grandma's "Be careful, now," I slid into the front seat alongside my uncle at the wheel, and with a wave to Grandma we were off. Slowly at first round the one or two corners to the end of the village, we emerged on to the road to Ferriby Sluice, and were soon bowling along the straight mile at 25 miles per hour. After the 10 miles or less per hour of horse travel, this was speed indeed. In an incredibly short space of time we were rattling over Sluice Bridge, and I remember giving a triumphant wave to Frank Straw, the lock-keeper, in his wide brimmed straw hat — no pun intended — who was standing near the bridge talking to a neighbour. We passed Sluice Farm on the right, and I noticed the garden gate and arch which my father had erected six momentous years previously.

Over the first switchback we zoomed with the overflow dyke on our left, and the Humber by the guard rail on the right, then over the second and third switchbacks, past The Grange, and we were in Winteringham village, where Uncle Joe had a call. While he was away I took a good look at the levers — brake and gear — the steering wheel with the throttle control at the side, and the two pedals. But most of all I was interested in that magical speedometer graded up to 60 miles per hour, surely a car could never travel at that incredible speed, 25 had seemed fantastic. Why, at such a speed it would be possible to cover the distance from South Ferriby to Sluice Lock in one minute!

While I was in this reverie my uncle returned, and we were on our way again, soon covering the intervening two or three miles to Winterton where he had to make a second call. While he was away I had time to reflect on the wonderful achievement of Henry Ford, the American who had brought such a marvellous instrument within reach of such as Uncle Joe. And, I thought, however long he is on his call, this car can never get restive and start to career down the road as the horse had done a day or two previously!

On our way back to Ferriby, we pulled up at Sluice Farm and went into the farmhouse for a quick chat with Aunt Sally and Uncle Fred. "Goodness, Bernie," my aunt said when she saw me, "How you've grown!" Then, "Could you do with a glass of milk?" Of course I could! And from the cellar she produced a glass of that delicious milk I always associated with Sluice Farm. Then, turning to Uncle Joe, she said with a moistness in her eyes, "If only his father had lived." I felt very embarrassed, but Uncle Fred broke the uncomfortable silence with, "Come and have a look at our new calf, Bernie." I went with him through the fold yard, past some clucking hens, and opening a door he pointed to a pretty little Ayrshire heifer calf, born only a day or two earlier. Its mother, tethered nearby, looked at us suspiciously and gave a low "Moo." We were admiring the dainty little creature when Uncle Joe appeared, saying it was time we were going. We said goodbye to the friendly couple at the garden gate, after Aunt Sally had given me a boiling of peas for "tomorrow's dinner."

Then we were on the last lap, and to my delight we speeded up to 30 miles per hour, while Uncle Joe told me that underneath the bonnet was an engine of twenty-two horse power. Never in my wildest dreams could I have imagined that sixty years later I should be driving my own car capable of 90 miles per hour on Britain's motorway network. However, in next to no time we were back at Grandma's, after a memorable outing, and she had to listen to my exciting account of what had been happening. This was the first of a number of drives in the Ford, all enjoyable, but none had quite the thrill of that first experience of motoring.

Some of my time was spent at the blacksmith's shop in the village High Street. The blacksmith was Harry Clark, and he was assisted by his two sons. The smithy had been in the hands of the Clark family since 1795, and fifty years after the events related here, Henry Clark, blacksmith, was still in the business, an extraordinary span of one family ownership approaching 200 years. 1914 was still the heyday of the horse for agricultural purposes, and the blacksmith had plenty of work shoeing the magnificent Shires and Suffolks.

During the holidays there were usually one or two boys hanging around the blacksmith's shop, and we enjoyed watching the glow of the smithy fire fanned by the hand-operated bellows, the fashioning of the shoe as the metal came white-hot from the fire, and the fitting and hammering on to the hoof with a sizzling and pungent smell. The horses, with owner or groom holding the bridle, always seemed to take this operation as a matter of course, and it was extremely rare to see one causing trouble. Occasionally Harry would let me "have a go" with the bellows, which was no doubt very good for my ego, and I loved listening to the village gossip, most of it good-natured, and interspersed with lively banter.

I mentioned earlier that Frank Andrew kept the village stores, also in the main street, and not far from the smithy. Some of my limited pocket money was spent there and I was rather partial to penny packets of kali, fizzy and sharp to the taste and very agreeable, but my favourite confectionery was a bar of Fry's Five Boy chocolate cream. The pictures of the boy on the packet showing his expressions from suspense to expectation and finally, satisfaction, were to my mind a clever example of advertising. My great-aunt Polly was the mother of the Andrew brothers, Frank, Will, and Harry, she being Grandma's sister, and a widow.

Still farther along the main street were the premises of "Cobbler" Bill, who was also a breeder of canaries, and his shop was lined with the cages of these birds. When they were all singing at once, there was a delightful medley of song. He had a relative, "Coin" Tommy (Smith) who made a hobby of collecting old coins. A Roman road, Middlegate, ran along the Wold escarpment above the village, by then grass-grown and little used, and many Roman coins had been found in its vicinity, most of them finding their way to Coin Tommy. At his death, he had a collection of over 2,000 coins, which were given to the Hull Museum.

Another family with whom we were very friendly were the Milners. They were distant relatives of ours, as indeed were so many of the villagers. Tom was farm foreman for gentleman farmer Harry Walker, and their house bordered the farm buildings where the eight Shire horses were stabled. Their son, Fred, was a few years older than myself, and through him I learned a lot about the agricultural scene as it was in those days, from making "bands," the twisted straw which was used to bind the corn into sheaves after being cut by the reaper, to the shooting of rabbits in the harvest fields. Binders, which not only cut the corn but tied it into sheaves, were only just coming into use, and village boys on holiday from school could earn a shilling a day making the bands which were soon to be superseded. Present day combine harvesters, which not only cut the corn but thresh the grain and bale the straw, were still over the distant horizon.

When a field of corn was being cut, the rabbits in the corn made for the diminishing uncut area in the centre, until as the last swathe was being mown, they made for the safety of the nearest hedgerow. Fred was a crack shot, and his double-barrelled gun usually got two or three rabbits. When harvesting was in progress, the odd rabbit frequently found its way to Grandma's table, and since harvesting coincided with my holiday, I naturally reaped the benefit.

The Milners' dwelling was a typical centuries-old farmhouse with long low ceilings, massive sideboard with rows of willow pattern plates, huge fireplaces and winding stairs. I used to be very interested in two big pictures which hung on the walls — one was the "Battle of Elteb" and the other the "Battle of Tel-El-Keber." Who the artists were, I have no recollection, but the action taking place in those two pictures fascinated me. They portrayed scenes from Britain's colonial struggles in the Victorian era, and the "Elteb" one reminded me of some of the lines so recently recited by Andy Wilson at Southcoates Lane School: "Red with the wreck of a square which broke, the Gatling's jammed and the Colonel dead and the regiment blind with dust and smoke....." only in this case the square was unbroken and the quadruple rows of redcoats were apparently giving a good account of themselves with rifle fire against the hoardes of natives hurling their spears and themselves into the fray. "Tel-El-Keber" was a mounted operation, and here, horses were rearing and swords were flashing as the helmeted mustachioed cavalrymen laid about the Dervish tribesmen.

These pictures with their animated scenes were a complete contrast to one which hung on the living room wall of Grandma's house, and which I very much admired. It was a peaceful scene of Scarborough's South Bay by moonlight, taken from the Spa, and it showed the mellow tones of the gas lamps reflected in the calm waters of the bay. Its date was probably mid-nineteenth century. I had never been to Scarborough, and thought what an attractive and romantic place it must be. Nearly forty years later, and after two world wars, our elder teenage daughter took a German pen-friend, who was staying with us, to Scarborough for the day. It was the German girl's first visit, and on their return to Hull, Waltraud declared that Scarborough was the most beautiful place she had ever seen.

Back to late July 1914, though, and one day I was playing a ball game with one of the village boys near the school which was closed for the holidays, when we heard the bell of the parish church start to toll. At slow and regular intervals the bell tolled ominously, and Albert said to me, "That means somebody's died." Just then a woman came round the corner and said, "Have you heard? Mr. Shrigley's dead."

Mr. Shrigley, you may remember, was the schoolmaster, and our last meeting was when he shook hands with Dorothy and me, five years earlier, and wished us success and happiness on our removal to Hull from Ferriby at the end of the July term in 1909. He had been schoolmaster for twenty years, and no-one in the village was more respected. Albert and I stood, stunned by the news, and listened as the bell continued to toll. I think it was fifty-seven times — the years of his age. He had died suddenly and unexpectedly while relaxing after a busy term.

This news cast a gloom over the village, which wasn't improved by the news that following the recent assassination of Archduke Francis Ferdinand, Austria had decalred war on Serbia, and that Russia was mobilising on the Austrian frontier. However, August Bank Holiday week-end was at hand, and this meant the annual Humber Sailing Club Regatta and Water Carnival which always took place on Bank Holiday Monday, and for which weeks of careful planning had been made, for this event was the highlight of the summer season.

Despite the news on Saturday, 1st August, that Germany had invaded Belgium as a preliminary to attacking France, Bank Holiday Monday found everybody who could manage it flocking to Ferriby Sluice. Some walked, many arrived by horse and trap, a few in cars, and others in wagonettes from places like Barton and Scunthorpe. It was a beautiful sunny day — August in England at its best — flags were flying, *Empress* and *Isle of Axholme* arrived packed with sightseers and anglers from Hull, and small sailing craft looked for moorings in the Haven.

The River Ancholme was a picture with houseboats and yachts, and picnic parties sat on the banks making inroads into the contents of their baskets and hampers. Ice cream vendors did a roaring trade. In the Humber, the sailing events took place one by one, and crack swimmers competed in the aquatic events, while the Hull City Police Band played popular selections on an improvised bandstand. The Greasy Pole competition produced roars of laughter as competitors tottered and swayed, before losing their balance and flopping with a splash into the salty water of the Haven. The final event was a competition for swimmers in which they had to catch mallards released in the water, but the birds were handicapped by having their wings tied. A bit of fun, but one hoped that the squawking mallards would be given a welcome release after being caught.

Then the crowds began to dwindle. *Empress* and *Isle of Axholme* took on board their hundreds of tired but happy holidaymakers bound for Hull, and

I with a party of friends enjoyed the leisurely walk up to South Ferriby. So ended a memorable last public holiday of a long era of peace, for the clouds of war were breaking, and no-one could imagine the consequences.

The greasy pole competition, Humber Sailing Club Carnival, Ferriby Sluice. 1914.

CHAPTER FOURTEEN

The events of the next day or two are well known, and indelibly written in the history books. Britain was pledged through the "Scrap of Paper" (the Kaiser's derisive term) to come to Belgium's aid if she were attacked. Germany, however, was bent on war — "Der Tag" had arrived — and Britain declared war on Germany at 11 p.m. on August 4th, as German troops poured into Belgium. I have two souvenirs of the period in the shapes of copies of the *Daily Mirror* for August 4th and 5th, 1914, given to me by a neighbour after he had finished reading them.

What had the *Mirror* to say on that portentious 4th August? "Let our attitude be one of visible calm and resolution, with no preliminary shaking of fists, and no undignified yelling against one side or the other. Destiny and fate lead us." And the headlines, very much smaller than those in use today: "British ultimatum to Germany," "French fleet in the Channel," "Plight of American Tourists." There were pictures of the fleet, of the crowds in Whitehall (the men all wearing boaters), Sir Edward Grey leaving the Foreign Office, and a German Zeppelin in flight.

Meanwhile sport was going on as usual. Against the Notts bowling, Jack Hobbs had made 226 for Surrey, who were heading the championship table. Lancashire had collapsed in the Roses match against the bowling of Drake and Wilfred Rhodes, and Steve Donoghue had won the 3 o'clock at Sandown Park on Agnate (6-1). *The Belle of New York* was having its long run at the Lyceum. Potash and Perlmutter were at the Queen's.

But I wonder how many people read the verse by Shelley headed "In Vain" at the bottom of page five on August 5th?

O cease! must hate and death return?
Cease! must men kill and die?
Cease! drain not to its dregs the urn
of bitter prophecy.
The world is weary of the past,
O might it die or rest at last!

I still had another ten days or so of holiday at Ferriby, and harvesting in ideal summer weather continued. I recall one incident, however, which was significant of the times. A couple of villagers had walked over to Barton-on-Humber, three miles away, for shopping, a day or two after war was declared, and I was in the village street when they returned. "Would you believe it," one said, "Sugar's gone up from 2d a pund to 6d, and flour's ayf-a-croon a ston." (It had been a shilling.) Panic shopping had produced panic prices.

Eventually the morning arrived for my return home, and I said goodbye to Grandma and various relatives and friends before boarding the *Ise of Axholme* for the hour's cruise over to Hull. When we passed the N.E.R.

Riverside Quay the scene around the terminal buildings was one of unusual activity. Groups of reservists and territorials in khaki uniforms were arriving with their kitbags by rail and road for transportation across to the continent to join the regulars who were fighting their heroic rear-guard action at Mons and Maubeuge.

Back home again, there were still several days before school restarted, and the Williams boys, George Ellams, Frank Whittaker and I spent our spare time playing cricket in the fields between Lee Street and the park. George's hero was his namesake George Hirst, but my man was Wilfred Rhodes. As I bowled left-handed and batted right-handed, we had that much in common. My last memory of the great Wilfred was nearly sixty years later, when as an old man in his nineties, and blind, he sat outside the pavilion at the Scarborough Cricket Ground at the annual festival, listening to comments on the match from colleagues, and reminiscing of bygone days.

There was, though, another field of interest now. Almost opposite East Park were the Territorials Barracks, the headquarters of the 4th Battalion of the East Yorkshire Regiment. In peacetime, a group of us would sometimes hang around the entrance, and occasionally get inside, to watch the Territorials on drill nights doing their squad drill and target practice. This used to give us quite a thrill, and the N.C.O.'s didn't seem to mind an audience; they perhaps looked on us as future recruits.

Now, however, it was different. The hall was a recruiting centre, and there was an air of quiet efficiency and some urgency, which brooked no dalliance with inquisitive schoolboys. Kitchener's call for a first "Hundred Thousand" was being answered in large numbers, and the drilling of raw recruits was taking place in the Hull parks. This was the time of the formation of the "Pals" batallions, and in Hull the "Commercials" were the first, groups of young men from offices joining to form what became the 10th East Yorkshires. They were quickly followed by the "Trades" who became the 11th East Yorks. Incidentally, the 5th — a pre-war battalion — were the "Cyclists" and they, or a company of them, would occasionally be seen in pre-war days, complete with rifles, cycling out into the country for manoeuvres.

My mother was rather shaken when her young brother, our uncle Joe Hollingworth, joined the Trades, and came round to see us wearing his red, white and blue armband. For us children, this meant the end of his periodic visits when he played cricket in the garden, or practised shooting at a gas mantle cardboard box dangling on a string attached to a washing line in the scullery. Our instrument was a spring-loaded pistol which fired a dart fitted with a rubber plunger. I had become quite adept at this harmless form of shooting, and with a steady hand and eye used to give Uncle Joe a good run for his money as far as target hits were concerned. However, this was now

Some of the Hull "Pals," 11th E. Yorks., drilling on the Hull cricket ground, October, 1914. Uncle Joe Hollingworth fourth from left, front row.

finished, as the 10th and 11th East Yorkshires were soon off to Pocklington for their first training camp.

On the day we assembled at school again, Tommy Mayman called us all into the Hall, and gave us a background picture of why we were in the war. At the end, we all received a booklet by Sir James Yoxall, the famous pre-war educationalist, on the ideals and aims of the British Empire, and the part we should play in this new situation.

Among those called up for active service was our cousin Stanley Heald, who was a Territorial in the Royal Artillery and nineteen years of age. His brother Arthur, two years younger, had been through the Trinity House School for the training of Merchant Navy officers, and was now an apprentice officer with a Liverpool based shipping line.

In the new school year, I was in Standard V, and by virtue of coming second in the previous year, had a desk on the back row next to Norman Smith, the number one. Our teacher was "Woodie," Mr. A. E. Wood, a competent teacher in his mid-forties, and also an artist of talent who had had a picture hung at the Royal Academy. One drawback to this, from our point of view, was that his standards of drawing and painting were extremely high. Consequently, his markings tended to be on the low side, and an effort for which another teacher might have given eight or nine out of ten, rarely gained more than seven.

It was Woodie who told us that Mr. Blackburn, who ran a men's tailor's and outfitter's business on Holderness Road, was giving away war maps of Europe, with index and flags of the Allies. Many of us made a bee-line for his shop to obtain one of these maps, which were in colour. I managed to get one before the supply ran out, and kept it for many years. Apart from its interest in showing where fighting was taking place on the various fronts, it provided a good background for a study to supplement our lessons on European Geography.

Our new classroom was in the eastern wing of the Senior Boys' School on the first floor of the block, and from my desk I looked over miles of open country towards the tall tower of Preston Church, and the even taller tower of Hedon Church, known as the King of Holderness. It was not until the mid-twenties that the building of the Southcoates housing estate, the first of several, began to restrict this view.

During that autumn term of 1914, the impact of the war was obvious, and it showed itself in the choice of popular songs. We were taught an English translation of the *Marseilles* at school. Most of us hadn't heard it previously, and I thought what an inspiring national anthem it was, much more exciting than our own sober *God Save the King*.

At the same time, the troops were route-marching through England and France singing *Tipperary* and *Pack Up Your Troubles* — indeed these two might almost have been the army's signature tunes. *Tipperary* also took on in

86

France, and over fifty years after the events related here I recall the enthusiasm of an elderly French audience at a holiday centre in Aquitaine when their English counterparts struck up this memory-provoking song, and the vigour with which they joined in with us.

Another song was soon being sung on every possible occasion. This was Ivor Novello's *Keep the Home Fires Burning*, which found a place in the nation's heart, and to me more than any other, recalls the spirit and the mood of 1914-15. One other which was very popular was *There's a Long, Long Trail*. At this time there was a craze at school for tin whistles, and nearly all the boys bought, begged, or borrowed one. They were quite cheap — even within my reach — and groups of us could be seen walking to school to the accompaniment of our tin whistles. We found the simple melody of *There's a Long, Long Trail* very easy to play, and Sculcoates boys were a familiar sight winding "into the land of their dreams" in step with the rhythm of this memory-tugging song, even if the singing of the nightingales was many miles away from East Yorkshire.

With most of us taking our tin whistles to school, one or another, as might be expected, couldn't resist the temptation to give a toot now and again when teacher's back was turned — great for us but not so good for discipline. If caught, the penalty was confiscation of the instrument and a caning, one on each hand, good and heavy. This eventually had the desired result and tin whistles remained stuffed inside jerseys during lesson time.

I must say here that canings were not done to excess, discipline was generally very good, and the heaviest punishments were reserved for lying and deceipt, or the justifiable complaints of nearby residents. Only once was I sent to the Head for caning. Norman Smith and I, with desks next to each other on the back row, got into the habit of having private jokes between ourselves, but we usually managed to keep a straight face when Woodie was looking in our direction.

On one occasion, though, and the point of the joke has gone from my memory, we were nearly exploding with merriment when Woodie caught us in the act. This served to make us almost hysterical, and we were nearly choking with ill-suppressed laughter, much to the amusement of the rest of the class. Pointing to the door, Woodie said, "Mr. Mayman's desk, you two — you'll soon be laughing on the other side of your faces — and tell him why I've sent you." Sobering up, we made our way to the sanctum, and explained our errand. Looking at us with his steely-blue eyes, in which I swear there was a ghost of a twinkle, he said, "Smith, Heald, you are the top two boys in Mr. Wood's class, and it's up to you to show an example to the others. If you can't behave yourselves what hope has the rest of the class."

He reached for his cane, and our spirits dropped to zero. "Hold out your left hands, both of you." We obediently held them out. Whack! on Norman's hand, then Whack! on mine. "Now the right hands." Whack!

Whack! "Go back to your places, and don't let me see you here again," he remarked. Apart from wincing, we didn't show any emotion, and walked back to our classroom with numb and aching palms. I thought of one of the Marfleet boys, a noted recalcitrant, who, a few days earlier, had received three on each hand for some rather serious misdemeanour, and realised why he had howled as the second and third strokes had descended. Norman and I never had occasion to visit the Head again on such an errard — perhaps we had learned discretion — but looking back and comparing modern permissiveness and uncontrolled hooliganism with the discipline of our day, I have no doubt in my mind which was the better training for life.

As the autumn term advanced, several of the staff enlisted, two of the first to go being Arthur Stuffins and a student teacher called Nicholson. Student teachers, just learning their craft, were normally "tolerated" by the boys, who regarded their sessions as periods of relaxation, but Nicholson was an athletic type and treated with respect. He was later killed in action — I believe on the Somme in 1916 — like so many of his generation.

To replace those who had gone to the war, one newcomer was "Tommy" Broad, who came out of retirement after a long teaching career which culminated in his headship at Mersey Street School which I had attended before coming to Southcoates Lane, as related earlier. He was tall and had a white short-trimmed beard. His face in repose had a rather serious look, and I used to compare him with my ideas of the prophet Elisha. Perhaps in this I was doing him an injustice, for I always associated Elisha with that incident recorded in the second book of Kings where the little children came out of the city and mocked him, saying, "Go up, thou bald-head," and in a fit of temper he cursed them, and she-bears came out of the wood and devoured them. For a "holy" man to act in this way I thought was disgraceful. Perhaps my ideas on the subject were coloured by an illustration of the prophet showing him with his balding head and white beard, which came up in a Sunday School lesson.

Tommy Broad took over Arthur Stuffin's class and whereas Arthur's teaching style was rather relaxed, his successor had a reputation as a very strict disciplinarian, and I was rather glad I had moved up before the change. I used to enjoy the music lessons, and although we learned the rudiments of Staff Notation, Tommy Mayman, who occasionally took us for music, was a great believer in Tonic-sol-fa, and usually played his flute from the latter. Songs that I remember learning were *Where the Bee Sucks, Pack Clouds Away, The Minstrel Boy* and *Sad Autumn Winds.*

I believe it was during this term that we had a series of lectures on "Alcohol and the Human Body." There were diagrams and pictures showing the effects of alcohol on the higher sensory parts of the brain, the blurring of moral guidelines, and the general slowing down of faculties which indulgence in alcohol caused. These lectures were obviously given with the approval of the City Education Committee, and if they did nothing else, they warned senior schoolchildren at a receptive time of their lives of the dangers in over-indulgence of alcohol.

On one occasion when Tommy Mayman descended on our class "to see how we were progressing," in this particular case, an arithmetic lesson, he showed us the advantages of adding up columns of figures in tens; e.g., instead of adding straight up, to look for 6's and 4's, 7's and 3's, 8's and 2's, 9's and 1's. Having once got used to this method, our additions were speeded up considerably, and in later life where figures loomed large, I often metaphorically thanked T.E.M. for introducing this method — a great time-saver. With the introduction of pocket calculators, the practice of quick mental additions has become almost a lost art. Parted from his pocket calculator, the modern youth faced with simple arithmetic seems rather helpless.

Most of us were keen collectors of cigarette cards, and probably made ourselves nuisances by making a beeline for anyone smoking a cigarette and calling out, "Cigarette card, please?" Some smokers, seen opening a new packet, might be almost swept off their feet by a group of urchins racing to be first to ask for the prized card. I gradually accumulated quite a collection, as Uncle Joe Hollingworth was a smoker, and most of his cards found their way to me. One of the pre-war series was "Army Life," and some of the scenes and routine operations contrasted strongly with the vast changes which the war was bringing about. For instance, there were scenes of the artillery horses being watered and fed, observation balloons being filled, cyclist sections reading maps, wounded being picked up by the R.A.M.C. and placed on horses' backs to be removed to field hospital, etc.

One of a series which came in with the war was "Gems of Belgian Architecture." These became rather poignant when such architectural masterpieces as Louvain Cathedral and Ypres Cloth Hall were destroyed in the fighting. Two 50-card sets which were great favourites of mine were "Overseas Dominions — Canada" and "Overseas Dominions — Australia." From a geographical point of view they were of good value, and the Canadian set showed such scenes as salmon fishing in British Columbia, felling trees and a lumbering camp, farming on the prairies, and a C.P.R. train entering the Rocky Mountains. From Australia, we had sheep-farming, rounding up cattle, mining quartz for gold, breaking in a horse, and catching turtles, together with fruit farming in Tasmania.

Another set which came out in late 1914 or early 1915 was a series of twelve reproductions of recruiting posters. These were excellent facsimiles in colour and caption of such famous posters as "The Scrap of Paper" (guaranteeing Belgium's neutrality, and signed for Germany by von Bulow), "Remember Belgium" (with a British Tommy on guard while a woman and child flee from their burning home), "He did *his* duty, will you do yours?"

89

(with a picture of the recently deceased Lord Roberts), "Fall In!" (with a khaki-clad bugler sounding the call), and "There is still a place in the line for *You*" (showing a line of soldiers with a place "reserved for a fit man."). There cannot be many complete sets of these reproduction recruiting posters in existence, but fortunately I kept mine.

My spare-time reading included R. M. Ballantyne, whose *Coral Island* I had found very absorbing, and after reading *The Dog Crusoe and His Master* I had an urge to go trapping and pioneering in Western Canada. The Williams boys were with me in this, and we used to meet in the "den" in their garden, complete with a table, a couple of old chairs, a stool, soapbox, shelf for odds and ends, and the floor was covered with a piece of old carpet. This constituted our "little grey home in the West." Not to be outdone though, I followed suit in my garden tool shed, with Dennis, now four and a half years old, as my No. 2.

Both hideouts were named "Klondyke Cabin" to perpetuate the story of the Klondyke gold rush in the Yukon, fifteen or so years earlier. In another wave of enthusiasm, my den became a wayside halt on the Alberta section of the Canadian Pacific Railway, complete with an old morse telegraphy tapper given me by Uncle Joe Hollingworth. I studied Morse Code, but never became very proficient at it. This was, of course, long before the introduction of wireless telephony, and the morse tapper was the means of communication on the railways before the telephone was in wide use.

CHAPTER FIFTEEN

Christmas arrived, preceded by the spurt to get all orders delivered on my baker's rounds, and this being the second Christmas delivering my loaves and cakes from the Misses Belt's oven, I had acquired more "sang froid" and did even better with Christmas boxes! My eleventh birthday was on December 20th, and to my great delight, my mother gave me a bow and a set of arrows for a birthday present.

Practising in the limited area of the garden was restricted, but later on I used to go with it into the fields behind the park, and even my critical friends were impressed by the range of that good little bow and its feathered arrows. Now, I could be either Robin Hood or an Indian brave, depending on the whim of the occasion. Harry and Reggie Williams had done equally well, having been given Indian Chief head-dresses and hatchets for Christmas presents. They were now Iroquois chieftains, greeting us with "How!" in as deep a voice as they could bring up from their boots!

Mother and we three children went to our grandparents Hollingworth for tea on Christmas Day. Uncle Joe had obtained Christmas leave and was there with his wife Hilda, looking very smart in his khaki uniform and puttees. The war, which at the start was "going to be over by Christmas," was in fact only just beginning, and I remember Grandma saying with a sigh that she wondered where we should all be when Christmas came round again. Alas, she herself died at the age of 76 between the two events, and Uncle Joe was two thousand miles away with his regiment, guarding the Suez Canal against possible Turkish attack, by late 1915.

A realisation that we in Hull were well and truly involved in the war came in June 1915, with the first Zeppelin raid. It was on the night of 6th June that a Zeppelin crossed the coastline and dropped bombs in several parts of Hull. At that time we had a young Methodist minister, Rev. Harry Edwards, occupying our spare bedroom. He was spending a short time in the Hull Kingston Circuit before taking up a post on the Mission Field in the West Indies, where he later spent many years serving his church in Jamaica.

Awakened by the bangs, we all came downstairs, and soon afterwards a neighbour ran down the street saying that the bombs had been dropped down Holderness Road near the Southcoates level crossing. Harry Edwards, who never wore a hat when hatless men were a rarity, and was a familiar figure in the district with his athletic stride, immediately set off to see if he could be of service. He was away several hours, and later on we heard that his presence in Waller Street, where several people had been killed and injured, had been of great value. Bombs also dropped in the Old Town had missed Holy Trinity Church by a few feet, but wrecked Edwin Davis's store nearby.

Following this raid, indignation in the city ran high. Shop windows were

A family group, 1915. Mother, self, Dennis, Dorothy.

broken where the owners were known to be of German origin, and accusations were made that they were spies in the service of the enemy. Demands were made for some protection against further attack, and the upshot was that before long a gun was mounted on the roof of Rose, Downs and Thompson's big foundry near Cannon Street Station. The sight of that long finger poking skywards gave an assurance to many Hull citizens in the weeks that followed.

Air raid warnings were introduced, and continued from time to time, but without any actual raids. The principal air raid hooter was the deep bass buzzer of Blundell, Spence's factory in Beverley Road. The ominous warnings in a series of short, deep blasts, sounded to some like the voice of doom, and it was always a relief to hear the long, happy note of the "All clear."

A system came into operation by which if the all clear came after 1 a.m., there was no school the following day, the idea being for the children to make up some of their lost sleep. It was not uncommon for groups of older children to cluster round their parents chatting in the street around 1 a.m., when some dad would scrutinise his watch and say, "Well, lads, it's after one o'clock." There would be a yell of delight, and shouts of "No school tomorrow!" In spite of these interruptions, lessons proceeded as normally as possible, but a new feature was the plotting of the Western Front positions on our European War Maps which showed the area in some detail.

Having reached the age of eleven, I was entitled during the summer and autumn terms to visit with my class in school hours, the East Hull Baths, and receive proper tuition in swimming. This was before the days of the "crawl" and we started with breast stroke, followed by the back and side strokes. We were not allowed to slide in, but right from the start had to dive in, in the approved style, but most of us started with "belly-floppers." Some boys panicked on their first attempts, and they were unceremoniously pushed in. I can't say I was too happy to begin with, but soon got used to it, and after a few lessons managed to scramble across the bath. Later on, I really enjoyed my swimming, but was never in the top rank.

Also in the summer sessions, Standard V started weekly visits to the Craven Street School's Handycraft Centre. Craven Street, being a Secondary School, had woodwork and metalwork rooms, unlike Southcoates Lane. The head of the handicraft section was a Mr. Armstrong, and older boys brought back spine-chilling tales of his ferocious temper, and ability to use his tools as weapons of offence against those who provoked him. So when our turn came to report at Craven Street — we marched from Southcoates Lane for a late morning session — we were filled with trepidation. "Woodie" introduced us, and then left us to the tender mercies of the "ogre," as some of them called him.

He was a man in his mid-fifties with fair hair beginning to grey, a florid complexion, hair sprouting from his ears, and prominent teeth. He looked us over, such as a slave trader or a member of the Spanish Inquisition might have done, or so we imagined, and then said, "You boys have come here to work, and I mean work; any slacking or fooling around will mean trouble. I stand no nonsense here, so let's make that quite clear from the start." He then took us to the woodwork room and introduced us to Mr. Thorpe. To our great relief, we learned that Mr. Thorpe was to be our tutor for woodwork, and it was only second and third year boys who were to study metalwork under the steely eye of Mr. Armstrong.

Mr. Thorpe was a much younger man, and was in fact later on called up for military service. His temperament was quite different from Mr. Armstrong. He showed us how to use the various planes, chisels and saws, and made the work interesting without any pressure or bullying. We thanked our lucky stars for not having to endure the pressure of his senior colleague. As previously, when undergoing the discipline of writing with my right hand, I found my golly-handedness a handicap, but by perseverence and restraining my desire to change tools to my left hand, I managed to keep my end up, and succeeded in making a few simple articles like dibbers and wall brackets. Occasionally we heard thumps and howling from the next door metalwork department, and when as sometimes happened, Mr Armstrong looked in and glanced at our work, we were model pupils on our best behaviour, and working industriously. Our year must have been favoured by providence, for when, twelve months later, we were due to receive the attentions of Mr. Armstrong for metalwork, he did a switch, and took the latest woodwork class himself, leaving a middle-aged newcomer to look after the metalwork, and us! So, mercifully, we evaded the physical complications which might have ensued, and were able to commiserate with our less fortunate brethren.

At the end of the summer term and the school year, when the marks were assessed, I found I had increased my aggregate, but, to my consternation, a dark horse in the shape of Clarence Bratley was two marks ahead of me, and indeed on level terms with the previously unassailable Norman Smith. This meant that I dropped to third place, and when Tommy Mayman came in to discuss with Woodie the markings, he said to me, "Tom, third place, what have you been doing?" I protested that my marks were up on the previous year, and with a ghost of a smile, he said, "Yes, but Clarence has done even better. However, let's see what you can do next time."

Third place entitled me to a prize, and a choice of books, if a somewhat limited one. Tommy Mayman recommended *The Cruise of the Gyrocar*, by Herbert Strang, just published, and detailing the adventurous journey from England to Constantinople (as it was then) by two young men who had invented a gyro-balanced two-wheeled motor car, which was also amphibious. They thwarted an international spy ring, and also prevented a

94

serious diplomatic incident, by delivering to its destination a highly secret document. I turned this book down, and later regretted it, in favour of *True to the Old Flag*, a story of the American War of Independence, by G. A. Henty. At that time I devoured every book of Henty's which I could get from the public library, and this one had eluded me. Later on, *The Cruise of the Gyrocar* came into the school library, and I was able to read what was a most fascinating modern adventure story.

The late summer and autumn of 1915 are memorable to me on account of three events, all tragic. In July of that year, while Germany and the Western Allies were more or less deadlocked on the Western Front, the Germans were attacking Russia in strength on the Eastern Sector, and to assist in their offensive had brought in for operations on the Baltic flank a number of battle cruisers from the High Seas Fleet. The Russians, who were in some difficulty, asked Britain for naval assistance, and the Admiralty sent into the Baltic four E class submarines. One of these, the E.13, went aground, and was discovered by a German unit which shelled the unfortunate submarine, killing many of the crew.

This incident, I believe, took place in neutral Danish waters, and caused much bitterness at the time. The bodies of the unfortunate sailors were brought back to Britain, via Hull, in a Danish cargo boat. They were landed at one of the Hull docks, and the fifteen or so coffins covered by Union Jacks were placed on gun carriages and conveyed in procession through the city centre to Paragon Station, from where they were transported to their home areas.

The procession took place on a Saturday morning, and as there was no school, a number of us made our way to the city, and took up positions on the route near what is now Queen's Gardens, but was then Queen's Dock. Soon we heard the strains of music, and round the corner from the direction of the Guildhall appeared a band of the Royal Marines playing Handel's Dead March in Saul. Behind the band was a squad of bluejackets marching in slow time with arms reversed, and then came the gun carriages, each one drawn by a section of sailors. As they passed where we were standing women wiped their eyes and men looked sadly at the flag-covered coffins. It was a most impressive and moving sight — even an eleven-year-old could feel the human tragedy behind the solemn pageantry, and learning something in the process.

The other two events were very different, but equally sad in their own special way. The eldest brother of my two friends Harry and Reggie Williams, as mentioned earlier, was Eddie. At the age of 17, a year previously, he had gone in for a proficiency test at National level organised by the Sea Scouts Section of the Boy Scouts Association. To the great delight of family and friends, and the local Scout officials, he had emerged with top marks throughout the country.

95

He was keen on a maritime career and, as a result of his success in the proficiency test, was awarded a grant, uniform, and an expense-free training course and apprenticeship in one of Britain's big maritime lines. I remember what a fine figure he looked in his mercantile marine apprentice's uniform before setting out on his first voyage.

His ship sailed for the River Plate, and it was while she was in a South American port that he contracted Yellow Fever, and died a few days later. When the news reached his parents, they were stunned and grief-stricken at the loss of their eldest son, and the end of what could well have been a long, happy and successful career.

But that was not all. A few days later, a number of cases of diphtheria occurred in East Hull. This was long before immunisation against such juvenile killers as polio and diphtheria was introduced, and once having contracted the latter, there was about a 50-50 chance of recovery. To the great distress of the Williams family and all who knew them, Reggie caught the disease, and a few days later, died on his eleventh birthday. I could hardly believe that my friend and sharer of so many childish exploits had gone, but for the Williams family who had lost two boys in a matter of weeks, it was devastating.

Back at school, selections were about to be made for candidates for possible scholarships to the Craven Street Secondary School, the Hull Grammar School and, for a few exceptionally brilliant pupils, Hymers College. The latter was a minor public school for boarders and day boys, founded in 1893 by John Hymers. Hull Grammar School goes back to Elizabethan times, and perhaps its greatest scholar was Andrew Marvell, poet, idealist, and friend of Milton, who was born at Winestead in Holderness in 1621, and died in 1678. He was the M.P. for Hull for nineteen years and lived through the momentous times of the Civil War, the Commonwealth, and the Restoration. Some of his poems are among the finest in English Literature, and one could mention *The Garden,* written at Nun Appleton when he was tutor to Lord Fairfax's daughter; *Cromwell in Death*, with its poignant opening, "I saw him dead: a leaden slumber lies, and mortal sleep over those wakeful eyes......" and *To his coy Mistress*, with its: "Had we but world enough, and time, This coyness, lady, were no crime" to ".....But at my back I always hear Time's wingèd chariot hurrying near, and Yonder all before us lie deserts of vast eternity....."

A charming novel entitled *Andrew Marvell and his Friends* was written by Hull authoress Marie Hall in 1874, and this shows not only a keen insight into Andrew Marvell's character, but gives a vivid description of the siege of Hull by the Royalist army in 1642. This book later became a firm favourite of mine, with its intimate details of life in Hull during the mid-seventeenth century.

But I am digressing. Tommy Mayman called me to his sanctum one day,

96

and said he would like to see my mother on the matter of me entering the scholarship examination. So the next morning, instead of romping through the fields to school, jumping ditches on the way, I walked sedately along via Sculcoates Avenue with my mother for company. Tommy, in his usual genial manner with parents, explained the position, and said that he thought I was a suitable candidate for a scholarship.

Then mother had to do what I'm sure was one of the most distasteful things in her life. This was to explain to the headmaster our precarious financial position. Nothing would have pleased her more, she said, than to allow me to go forward for selection, but circumstances were so difficult that it was really quite impossible to consider the extra years' schooling which would be necessary. As she had been a teacher herself before marriage, one could appreciate what this must have cost her. Tommy Mayman was very understanding, and said he could appreciate the difficulty, but regarded it as a great pity. "However," said he, "Boys from Southcoates Lane usually do very well on leaving school, and prospective employers seem to go for our pupils, while there are always evening classes for further education." So that was that, and I had to swallow my disappointment.

When the list of successful candidates came through later, Norman Smith had gained an entrance to the Hull Grammar School, while Clarence Bratley was accepted for the Craven Street Secondary School. Some years after the end of the war, Craven Street became the Malet Lambert High School in fine new premises overlooking the East Park and its lake.

With the continuing shortage of teachers — two more had left for the Forces — some telescoping was necessary, and the top dozen or so in Woodie's class were moved up to "Pa" Hudson's Standard VII, and the highest class in the school. Most of us who moved up were just over twelve years of age, and in doing this we missed the intervening class presided over by Mr. Simpson. "Simbo" looked after the sports side of the school's activities, and had been instrumental in raising the football team to its outstanding position in the local schools' competitions.

Pa Hudson was a dour looking man in his late forties, and had received his nickname by virtue of having two of his own boys at the school, both of whom passed on to higher education. He had a reputation for standing no nonsense, and was the deputy Head, but we new boys to his class were given a very fair introduction, and I think the stories of his severity were greatly exaggerated.

He had a keen sense of humour behind his dour exterior, and the not quite eighteen months I spent under him were probably the happiest of my short school career. Classes at that time were never less than 50, and frequently were in excess of 60 boys, yet the teachers seemed able to cope and achieve good results. The stricter discipline of those days certainly helped, and any signs of insubordination were quickly nipped in the bud. It was a far cry from

97

the "free expression" today with its demoralising effect on teaching staffs and resultant low educational standards.

Having earlier received a good grounding in English grammar, history, geography, arithmetic, and the rudiments of chemistry, with a little art and music, we were now able to go in for algebra, geometry, world geography, and some self-expression in art. Pa Hudson had a flair for teaching and conducting choral music, and he possessed a little reed about two inches long from which he obtained the key of C — the only piano on the school premises was in the school hall. His singing lessons were always welcomed, and he was able to draw out of us the musical expression which he desired.

1916 was a momentous year in many respects. The fairly lengthy period without any Zeppelin raids came to an end on Sunday, March 5th. It had been snowing intermittently during the day, and by nightfall the countryside was white over. Not long after dark, the ominous notes of the air raid warning buzzers were heard, and for a while nothing more happened. Our family sat around talking, or trying to read by the aid of a couple of candles — mother had turned off the gas — and we were beginning to think that this was another of the warnings without a subsequent raid, when around 9 p.m. we heard the distant, characteristic high-pitched beat of Zeppelin engines. My family and our next door neighbours shared a covered concrete passageway between the houses, and we had agreed to use this as an air raid shelter, so when an alarm sounded, an old carpet was put down and blankets arranged, so that a quick exodus could be made from the houses.

Putting out our candles, we quickly made for the passageway, as the engine beats got louder. A few minutes later, we heard the "Crump! Crump!" of falling bombs exploding quite some distance away. After a brief interval, there it was again, and yet again, with apparently no reply from our anti-aircraft gun on Rose, Downs foundry roof. At the height of the raid, our next door neighbour's daughter, a girl of about 17, became hysterical and could not be quietened. At length, her father sought to give her a swig from a bottle of brandy which he kept handy, and in the darkness and confusion mistook my sister Dorothy for her, and tried to force the brandy down Dorothy's throat. She screamed and fought against these attentions, and "Dad" kept saying, "Now, now, dear, this will help you; now be a good girl and drink up. Come on, dear, it will do you good." Pandemonium reigned for some minutes until things were sorted out! Later on, we had some good laughs over this incident, and Dorothy's leg was pulled on many occasions. In fact, I can recall my mother and sister being almost hysterical themselves as I mimicked the role of the good neighbour with the aid of a lemonade bottle and Dorothy's unwilling mouth!

However, back to the more serious matter of the air raid. At last, the sound of explosions ceased, and I remember stealing out into the snow-covered street, and seeing dimly against the star-lit sky, a cigar-shaped raider making for the coast.

After what seemed an eternity, the welcome note of the air raid relief sirens was heard, and we rather wearily made our way back into the house again, where mother made us a cup of tea. While we were relaxing over our tea, and wondering what had befallen those unfortunate people in the direct track of the bombs, our grandfather clock, which stood in a corner of the living room, struck two o'clock, I think it was. This clock, made at Guisborough in North Yorkshire, had been in the family for about 150 years, and had gone with the Dawsons to South Ferriby when they had moved there from Great Ayton in the eighteen-thirties. Winding up the clock was mother's last job before going to bed, and this was achieved by pulling on a chain through which a system of gearing raised an extremely heavy iron weight from near floor level to just below the clock face. "Grandfather" sounded the hours in extremely loud and compelling tones as a hammer struck the bell, preceded by a gutteral warning tone which prepared listeners for the rather ear-piercing clang!

After a few hours sleep, daylight came, and with it the assessing of the damage to life and property. Damage was widespread, but the area around Paragon Station was the worst hit, Collier Street and the densely populated district of nearby Anlaby Road being the worst affected. Many people had lost their lives, and others were homeless. This, the "Snowy Sunday Night" as it came to be called, was never forgotten by those who had lived through it.

Inevitably came the question, what was the gun on Rose, Downs' foundry doing during the raid? Then came the bitter truth — it was a dummy gun! The people of Hull had been hoodwinked, and the city seethed with indignation. Questions were asked in the House of Commons by the local M.P.s, and a demand was made for real protection. The angry populace was in no mood for half measures, and the result was that four properly equipped A.A. sites were established round the city from Marfleet in the east to Dairycoates in the west.

Nevertheless, many people felt that the best chance of safety lay in getting out of the city into the countryside, and when subsequent air raid alarms came they could be seen trekking along the main roads out of the town, family by family. Mothers pushed perambulators containing their babies and precious belongings, while father — if not at the war — carried toddlers in blankets or looked after the older children, a sad sight indeed. It should be remembered that, unlike the 1939-45 war with its limited warning periods, there was usually a two hours or so interval between warnings and actual raids, Zeppelins by comparison with modern planes being extremely slow moving, and Naval Intelligence usually had the airships plotted before they were halfway across the North Sea.

The next actual raid came three months later, on the night of 6th June. Again, the air raid warning and the long wait. Then once more the high-pitched note of Zeppelin engines, but this time we heard the bark and whine of A.A. shells as the barrage opened. What a contrast to the March raid! Some of us ran into the street to see what was happening, and then, boy, oh boy! we saw two searchlights raking the sky suddenly latch on to a Zeppelin high in the sky. There it was, a silver cigar, caught in the searchlights, with pin-points of fire like tiny fireflies showing where the A.A. shells were bursting around it.

With a weaving movement, the Zeppelin dropped its load of bombs in open fields, gained height, and disappeared seawards. Sometime later, the all clear sounded, and we heard afterwards that the raider had been destroyed over the North Sea. Defence was catching up with attack, and although odd raids continued, quickly repulsed, never again was there the devastation of March 5th, 1916.

A primitive form of black-out was in existence, with all the street gas lamps covered blue, except for a small clear area near the bottom. One had then a ghostly illumination for a few yards underneath the blueness, plus a small pool of dim light directly underneath. I mentioned earlier that the various tram routes were distinguished by big letters on the front and rear of the vehicles, Holderness Road being "H." Now, it was a most peculiar coincidence that when, after dark, the letters were illuminated by a shaded electric bulb, Lord Kitchener's features came through the lines of the "H" with great clarity. Who first spotted the likeness, I have no idea, but there is no doubt at all that there was a most remarkable resemblance to the war leader who at that time was held in almost as much reverence as Winston Churchill was to be in World War Two. It might indeed have been an illuminated photograph, complete as it was with his famous moustache and those grave, penetrating eyes, so striking was the resemblance. This feature was noticeable only on the Holderness Road "H" letter boards, not on any other route.

At this time, men above military age were being invited to join the "Volunteers," fore-runners of the Home Guard of World War Two. I used to watch a squad of them drilling in the East Park from time to time, using broom handles for rifles. Some of them, men in their fifties and early sixties, seemed to make heavy weather of their unaccustomed exercise, their pronounced middle-aged spread proving rather a handicap, but probably most of them benefited physically. Later, they were provided with blue-grey uniforms and looked quite smart. No doubt they had the satisfaction of feeling that they were doing something for their country in a critical period.

By now, my brother Dennis and his namesake, the youngest of the Williams boys, had started school in the Infants' Department at Southcoates Lane, and they joined the contingent from Lee Street trekking across the fields to "Southcoates" daily. The Girls' Department was presided over by a Miss Sweeting, a lady getting on in years, whom I later compared with Margaret Rutherford who starred as the schoolmistress in *The Happiest Days of your Life*. A new recruit to the Senior Boys' Department was a Miss Waller, just out of her student days. A charming person, and very pretty into the bargain, she was regarded as a welcome addition by both staff and pupils!

CHAPTER SIXTEEN

The much debated Battle of Jutland took place on 31st May / 1st June 1916. Was it a victory for us, or for the Germans? Both sides claimed it, but each suffered heavy losses, and the sinking of battle cruisers like the *Queen Mary* and *Invincible* with many casualties was a heavy blow to us. Weather and tactics had a good deal to do with the result, and Beattie's Battle Cruiser Squadron with their lighter armament took the brunt of the attack by the battleships of the High Seas Fleet, before Jellicoe's main battle fleet arrived on the scene. If the latter had been within range in time, there is little doubt that few of the German ships would have survived, but as it was, the North Sea mists enabled the Germans to elude Jellicoe, and they slipped away to the safety of their home base at Wilhelmshaven. I suppose we have every right to claim a victory, as the German High Seas Fleet never appeared again until the war was over, when they emerged from their anchorage to sail to Scapa Flow where they were ignominiously scuttled.

The news that a big naval battle had taken place in the North Sea was soon circulating in Hull before the official bulletins were issued, and several of our damaged ships limped into the Humber for repair and refit, among them being the destroyer *Chester*. Most people will have heard the story of Jack Cornwell, boy telegraphist on the *Chester*, who stayed at his post during the height of the battle, although mortally wounded. He had been a boy scout in Grimsby, and his name became a legend in the Scout movement. He was awarded a posthumous V.C. and the Boy Scouts Association instituted an award for bravery in his honour. A "Jack Cornwell" ward in memory of this Grimsby boy was founded at the Star and Garter Home for incapacitated ex-servicemen at Richmond, Surrey, and when the full story of his heroism was made known, stickers bearing his picture in uniform, one of which I still possess, were on sale in aid of the fund. I shall always remember travelling on the top of a tram along Hedon Road, and seeing the battered *Chester* with all her battle wounds, undergoing repairs in Alexandra Dry Dock, only a few feet away from the main highway.

When we broke up for the summer holidays in July, the Battle of the Somme was at its height. Starting on July 1st, casualties, as is well known, were fearful. The West Yorkshire "Pals," mostly from Leeds and Bradford, suffered great losses in the early days of the battle. The turn of the Hull "Pals" was to come a little later on. In the meantime, Uncle Joe Hollingworth had ended what he later described as a very agreeable and cushy interlude. Little activity had occurred there, and he had had the opportunity to visit the Pyramids and Sphinx during his leave periods. He had now been transferred to the 13th East Yorkshires, another of the "Pals" batallions, and this unit had moved from Alexandria to France via Marseilles, to take up positions on the Somme front.

The East Yorkshires went "over the top" on the 13th November during the Battle of the Ancre, a follow-up to the Somme. On that day, several battalions of the East Yorkshires attached to the 50th Division attacked the village of Serre, strongly held by the Germans. Dreadful losses were sustained, and for many Hull families it was the blackest day of the war. For years afterwards, on the anniversary of that day, the "In Memoriam" section of the *Hull Daily Mail* had a special page for the hundreds of names of those who had given their all. I remember Uncle Joe's wife coming to see us in some distress a day or two later, and she was carrying a postcard she had received from the War Office stating that Private J. J. Hollingworth was in base hospital, having been wounded in action. This set us all wondering if the injury was serious, and it was a great relief when the facts became known later. It appeared that while Joe was going over the top, he had received a machine gun bullet wound in his right hand, incapacitating him from further action. He was one of the fortunate ones, for when the wound healed there was still partial incapacity, and he was put into a non-combatant unit for the rest of the war. This type of injury was usually described by the troops as a "blighty."

However, prior to this digression, we were breaking up for the summer holidays. A disappointment was in store for potential school prize winners when Tommy Mayman came round to tell us that owing to wartime economy measures the Education Committee had decided that awarding and distribution of prizes had been discontinued for the duration of hostilities. This was particularly disappointing for me, as I learned that I would have qualified for the form geography prize if times had been normal.

Holidays meant South Ferriby again for a couple of weeks, renewing friendships with village boys I had come to know earlier, and visiting relatives. As usual I stayed with Grandma in her cottage, for what was to be the last time. One of the boys, a year or two older than I was, had a sister called Eileen, a few months younger than myself. Now 12½, I had previously taken little notice of girls, regarding them rather as some sort of inferior males who were hopeless at games, at any rate our sort of games, and had no idea how to handle a ball.

However, I suddenly realised how pretty Eileen was with her blue eyes and freckles, and hair done in plaits. The trouble was, I felt completely tongue-tied when I was in her company, particularly if she was alone, and usually made some excuse for leaving, then felt like kicking myself for being so foolish. This little flash of awareness of the other sex though did not prevent me from enjoying myself in games with the village boys when time off from harvesting allowed.

One of our diversions was to go down to the Humber shore for bathing and practising ducks and drakes with the plentiful supply of flat, chalky stones which formed the "checkers" beach. Another favourite was playing hide and seek in the Woodland bordering Ferriby Cliff. "Cliff" was a quarry where the local chalk was removed from the hillside site by blasting, and a narrow gauge railway took the little wagons loaded with chalk down a narrow ravine to a jetty on the Humber about half a mile away. Here, keels and barges were moored, and the chalk was shot down a chute into the holds for conveyance to the Barton-on-Humber cement works, or another cement works situated on the River Hull. Alternatively, the chalk could be used for ballast for road schemes.

At week-ends, or evenings when the working had stopped, the place was a happy hunting ground for the local youth. Tampering with equipment was strictly forbidden, and on no account was any interference allowed with the trucks on the various sidings. As the narrow gauge track was down an incline to the jetty, any trucks with brakes released and unattended would gather momentum and crash into or through buffers at the other end, with a possibility of serious injury and damaged equipment. I never saw any foolishness or hooliganism, but I believe accidents happened at times. The woods were the home of foxes, and it was not uncommon if walking along the track between the village and the quarry to hear the barking of these animals in the bordering scrubland. Bird-nesting was a common pastime, all the usual woodland birds being found here, and I'm afraid not all the collectors followed the ornithologists' advice to take only one egg from each nest.

Grandma's health was perceptibly failing, but she was still as bright as ever. I made myself as useful as possible by doing jobs around the house, weeding the garden, and going errands as required.

Over on the Yorkshire side of the river, exciting things were happening at Brough, easily seen from South Ferriby and other points on the Lincolnshire side. Recently the Blackburn Aeroplane Company of Leeds had built an establishment on the level land near Brough Haven, with hangers and air strip. They were busy building planes for the war effort in France, and, with a river frontage, were starting to build seaplanes.

These canvas and wood machines of 1916 were frail and flimsy by modern standards, but to see them in the air from our grandstand position over the waterway was really thrilling. There were also one or two semi-rigid airships which I think were being developed for spotting enemy submarines in the coastal approaches. These airships looked quite sensational to me as they travelled slowly at a height of perhaps 500 feet above the water, turning and manoeuvring.

The airship saga is a story in itself, but Germany, through Count von Zeppelin and his work at Friedrichshafen on Lake Constance, had taken a big lead in lighter-than-air development, which we never caught up. Five years after the events related here, I was to see the R38 cruising down the Humber in August 1921 on a proving flight before being sold to the United States as the ZR2. When off Hull Corporation Pier, the envelope sagged, broke in two, and the big airship burst into flames, the wreckage falling into the estuary. It was a mercy that the doomed aircraft missed the densely populated area of the Old Town by a few hundred feet, or the loss of life could have been dreadful. As it was, forty-four lives were lost, and there were only five survivors.

Still later, in October 1929, I went over to Howden near Selby to see the privately built R100 in her huge hangar at Spaldington, and was shown round the super-airship before her successful flight to Canada. The vastly increased strength of her lattice-work girders over those of the ill-fated R38 was pointed out; one sat in the comfortable arm-chairs in the lounge, and admired the purposeful kitchen with its aluminium fittings. A walk along the promenade deck, inside the structure but with vast perspex windows, gave an indication of the treat in store for future passengers. However, the disaster to the cousin of the R100, the R101 — government constructed at Cardington — on her maiden voyage to India, when she crashed at Beauvais in France and was completely destroyed, put an end to airship construction and development in England. Sadly, the R100, pride of Yorkshire, was broken up for scrap, a fate she never deserved. The story of the construction of these two airships is told in Nevil Shute's book *Slide Rule,* and he pin-points the differences between the situations at Cardington and Howden. Interference by government officials at Cardington, constant changes in planning details, and a rigid determination to have the R101 in the air for a prestige flight to India on 4th October 1930, come what may, is contrasted with Barnes Wallis and his team at Howden who were able to apply their skills with quiet efficiency, and without the frustration of officialdom which the Cardington men had to put up with. So the much publicised flight of the R101, under-powered and with a leaky envelope, ended in a steep dive to death a few hours after leaving Cardington. Of the fifty-four persons on the ship, only six survived, and among the victims was the Minister for Air, Lord Thomson.

After returning home from South Ferriby, and before the next school term began, I had several exciting visits to our cousins, the Turners, who had taken a cottage at Willerby for a few weeks. George, who as mentioned earlier was the same age as I was, had recently received a bicycle, and had just learned to ride it. I was very keen to learn, and he and I used to go to Castle Hill between Willerby and Skidby, on the edge of the Wolds. George rode his bicycle from the village, with me on the backstep, until we came to the top of Castle Hill. Here, we took it in turns to go down the gentle slope which gradually steepened. I soon got the knack of balancing, and we had some exhilarating times, freewheeling down the hill and scooting up the next slope to Skidby Windmill, then reversing the process.

At that time, this section of roadway was just a country lane, and we could enjoy our antics with no traffic to bother us — it was most unusual to come across another vehicle. The road is now the A164 from Hessle to Beverley and carries very heavy traffic which would make our fun and games impossible today.

It was not long after these excursions that I was given a bicycle by my father's eldest brother, William, who had a drysaltery business in the Wilmington area near the wharves of the River Hull. It was an Alldays machine which he had used for some time, but was in good condition. The trouble was that it had a 26 inch frame, Uncle Will being a tall man, and when I attempted to ride it I was faced with a problem. My legs were not long enough to reach the pedals! I could make some sort of progress by jerking the pedals forward and then back-pedalling, but serious cycling was out of the question until I grew longer legs. It was mother's elder brother Tom who supplied the answer when he visited us about a week later. "I'll make you some wooden blocks," said he, "And fix them to your pedals." He made and fitted these, and I was then able to use the machine without difficulty.

Now I was able to escape from the built-up areas, and get out into the nearby countryside. First, second, and third Sutton Lanes (now Ings Road, Bellfield Avenue and Salthouse Road), all leading to the village of Sutton, were the first essays in exploration on two wheels. Later on, Bilton, Sproatley, Skirlaugh and the sylvan delights of Burton Constable Woods came into my orbit. I kept that bicycle for the next five years, and the quiet hum of the tyres on macadam roads, or the crunching on gravelled lanes became sweet music.

This "Alldays Special" was eventually passed down to Dennis when I became the proud possessor of a lightweight machine with laminated wooden wheels, North Road bars, and Eadie Coaster Hub, at the age of 17. By then I was travelling much farther afield, and the whole of the East Riding was within my compass.

It was in 1916 that conscription was introduced. The flow of recruits for the forces under the voluntary system was falling off, and I remember a major recruiting campaign with massed bands parading the city, which yielded only fifty recruits — a big disappointment for the military promoters. It was realised by the government that the appalling losses in the war of attrition on the Western Front could not be replaced without compulsory military service. I had a second cousin at South Ferriby who had rejected all recruiting blandishments. Harold Dawson had said, "If they want me they'll have to come and fetch me." Something of an idealist, he hated the thought of war and the killing involved, but would not register as a conscientious objector. Whether he had a premonition of disaster, I don't know, but called up under conscription, less than six months later he was killed by a bursting shell on his first appearance in the trenches on the Western Front, leaving a wife and two little boys, one of whom died shortly

106

afterwards. The other, named Harold after his father, died when 37 years of age. Yet strangely enough, his mother lived to be over 90, having been a war widow for nearly sixty years, and outliving all of her own generation.

At home, our domestic affairs were reaching a situation which I viewed with misgivings, if not indeed, alarm. With wartime price increases affecting the cost of living, our economic situation was, if not desperate, very tight, and further means of assisting the family budget were being looked for. At that time there was an arrangement under the educational system whereby children who had attained a certain standard of education could leave school before reaching the statutory age of 14. The candidates had to undertake what was called the "Labour" examination, and, if they passed, could be released after about the age of 12¾.

I was now in Standard VII — the top form at school — and occupying a high position in class. My mother reasoned that if I stayed until I was 14, teaching would be mainly repetition, and I would be better employed helping the family's finances. Selfish though it may seem, this wasn't the way I looked at it, for I was enjoying school immensely. The geography of far-flung places fascinated me, and the school atlas was almost my bible. History, too, had its special place, and I was keenly interested in English history following the Norman Conquest. I had recently read Bulwer Lytton's *Hereward the Wake* and greatly admired the stand, hopeless though it was, of those English patiots like Hereward, Gospatric and Waltheof, who refused to accept William of Normandy. I have often wondered what the course of our history might have been if Harold had won at Senlac Hill, as indeed he could well have done had his army not had to face an exhausting march of two hundred and fifty miles after defeating Harald Hardrada and Tostig at Stamford Bridge. History, though, is full of ifs and buts, and another interesting conjecture is the course of events if the much maligned — some would say unjustly so — Richard III had won the Battle of Bosworth in 1485, instead of his opponent, Henry, Earl of Richmond, who ushered in the Tudor dynasty. Could a continuation of the Plantagenets have matched the late flowering of the Tudors in the shape of Elizabeth and the Elizabethen Age?

Back, however, to the immediate problem as far as I was concerned. I have long contended that one never stops learning, and in the relaxed atmosphere of Standard VII under Pa Hudson's benevolent leadership behind his dour exterior, I was feeling the benefit of earlier grappling with grammar, tables, angles and dates. Essay writing had become a pleasurable pastime, and even maths had lost its unattractiveness. So to put things mildly, I viewed the prospect of leaving with dismay, particularly as I had not yet attained my thirteenth birthday.

My mother arranged an interview with Tommy Mayman, and again told him of our financial difficulties. He was most sympathetic, and said how

107

greatly he regretted the circumstances. Yes, there was little doubt that I could pass the Labour Examination, and he would put me in for the next one, which would be in mid-October. That ominous day arrived far too quickly, and how I hated it. I went along to the central school where the examination was being held, and joined the thirty or so others on the same errand. Some were obviously looking forward to their "escape" from school, but for me it was as if I had passed through the dismal portals into some sort of condemned cell.

Examinations papers were passed round, and I looked at mine dully. There was a feeling of unreality about the whole business, as if it was some sort of nightmare from which I should eventually wake up to find it had been only a dream. I wrote down some semblance of answers in a mechanical way, but my mind was in a haze of incomprehension.

At last, the papers were collected and we were free to go. I went home, and was very uncommunicative when my mother asked how I had fared. It was a relief to escape to the baker's, and get on to my bread round. At least, this took my mind off the immediate past events, and gave me something else to think about.

A few days elapsed, and then one morning I was called to the headmaster's desk. He looked at me seriously for a moment, without speaking. then, "Heald," (not Tom), he said, "You've failed." I had half expected the result, but when it was confirmed with such awful certainty, I felt utterly ashamed and stunned. "What happened?" he said. I almost burst into tears, but just managed to control myself. Then I told him that I never wanted to pass, and hadn't really tried, that I loved school and wanted to stay on as long as possible. He was very understanding. If he had shown too much sympathy I should probably have broken down. If, on the other hand, he had given me a good dressing down, it would have fanned the flames of resentment against the whole wretched and melancholy business. Instead, he just said he knew exactly how I was feeling, but that this was a challenge. Difficulties were there to be overcome, and opportunities had to be grasped.

After a slight pause, he said he would enter my name for the next Labour Exam in three months time. "Let them see what you are made of, Tom," he remarked. "I know, and you know, that you can do it and be a credit to the school." I felt quite a lot better after this, and more able to face the situation when I got home. Mother was very disappointed, but cheered up when I told her that there was another chance in three months time, that I had got the hang of the questions, and felt confident that I should pass on the next occasion.

The next few months passed far too quickly. I had my thirteenth birthday, Christmas came and went, and at school we had what was my last carol concert, and one that I remember for our singing of the carol *Like silver lamps in a distant shrine,* which I have heard only very infrequently since. Every now and then, we had visits at school from old boys on leave — the 13-year-olds of 1912 were now 18 years of age, and liable for military service. Strapping figures they were in their khaki uniforms and puttees, most of them wearing the badge of the East Yorkshire Regiment, and soon to face the horrors of trench warfare in the never ending mud and anguish of Flanders.

In early February came the notice to attend Labour Examination No. 2. I had had my three months respite, and was reconciled to leaving school and all its friendly associations. The last weeks had been most agreeable, and Pa Hudson, who knew all about my circumstances, was kindness itself. He wished me luck on the day of the exam, and said, "You'll do it all right, son, but tackle the easiest questions first."

In the event, I had no difficulty with the questions, and finished the paper before some of the candidates were more than half-way through. I handed my paper in, and walked out into the sharp air again feeling, "That's that." Again the few days of waiting, and then the visit to Tommy Mayman. He was smiling when I walked up to his desk. "Well, Tom," he said, "You've managed it this time. I thought you would. Now, what are your plans?" I told him that I was interested in ships and shipping, and wondered if there might be a chance of getting into the offices of Thomas Wilson, Sons & Co. (Later, this was Ellerman's Wilson Line). The red and black funnelled ships of the Wilson Line were a familiar sight on the River Humber, and as well as a busy continental trade, their bigger vessels sailed to the Mediterranean, America, and the Far East. "There's quite a lot of scope with Wilson's," said the headmaster. "Your best plan is to go along to see Mr. Elliott, their staff manager; take your reference, and tell him I suggested you went to see him. I'll let Mr. Hudson know you will be leaving at the end of the week. Come and see me on Friday afternoon, Tom, and I'll give you your school reference."

I passed the next few days in a bit of a daze. I was now eager to see what the next chapter had in store, and yet sad to leave Southcoates Lane with all the companionships I had made there over the last five years. Morning assembly, the lessons, the playtime fun, the sports, the concerts, the integrity of the staff led by an outstanding headmaster who had shown great insight into what made boys tick, had all blended into a tradition which was to be a treasured possession of those fortunate enough to be counted among the "swallows" of Southcoates Lane. One is tempted to quote Shakespeare and say, "We few, we happy few, we band of brothers....."

Friday afternoon came, and I put pens, exercise books and text books away for the last time. Pa Hudson wished me well, and Tommy Mayman handed me my reference — or "character" as most school-leavers called it.

It read as follows:

Hull Education Committee.

Southcoates Lane Boys'

HULL, 23rd Feby 1917.

Thomas Bernard Heald
of 34 Lee St. has attended
the above school since 8·1·12.

He is a boy of good abilities
and Excellent character. He is
well behaved, quiet in manner
obedient & hardworking.

He is thoroughly reliable
and trustworthy & will give
his employers every satisfaction. I am sorry to lose
him.

T. E. Mayman
Head Teacher.

CHAPTER SEVENTEEN

The next week-end passed with the usual routine, household jobs and the bread delivery round on the Saturday, Sunday School on Sunday afternoon, with a bit of reading in between times, and a chat with my friend Harry Williams, who at sixteen was now a solicitor's junior clerk. I had to tell the Misses Belt that they would soon need a replacement for the baker's round which had been mine for over three years.

On Monday morning it seemed strange to see Dorothy bustling off to her office, and Dennis getting ready for school, while I was in a sort of limbo, no school, and no job as yet. On the Tuesday I went with my mother to the offices of the Wilson Line to be interviewed by Mr. Elliot. We took a tram to the city centre, and walked along Waterhouse Lane and Commercial Road until we came to the big red-brick building which housed the offices, just before the "T" Bridge where the road crossed the railway to Wellington Street and the Albert Dock lock-pit. The rattle of horse-drawn rullies piled high with merchandise mingled with the sound of shunting at the approach to the Kingston Street Goods Station nearby.

Entering through the heavy swing doors, my mother explained our business to the enquiry clerk, and we were shown into a small room, and told that Mr. Elliot would see us shortly. In the meantime I had a quick glance round the main office, and saw dozens of desks and partitioned-off sections which housed little groups of clerks examining papers, writing, or answering the shrill call of the telephone.

After a few minutes, Mr. Elliot came in. He was a tall, grey-bearded man, and wore a frock coat, black of course, a choker collar and grey tie. My mother explained our errand, and introduced me. I produced my reference, and mentioned that Mr. Mayman had suggested we see him. He scanned the reference, asked a few questions, and heard something of our background. He said that they hadn't a vacancy just then, but I would be put on their list. In the meantime, he said, he knew of a firm of average adjusters in High Street who required a boy, and if we went along to see them, mentioning his name, I should probably get the position and be able to work there until the next Wilson Line vacancy, which would be notified to us.

The interview over, we retraced our steps to the city centre, and walked through Whitefriargate to High Street, which was full of buildings and chambers housing solicitors, accountants, merchants, and transport concerns. The average adjusters we had been told of occupied premises which, to me, looked dark and dismal in the extreme, with only an apology for daylight percolating through the inadequate windows. I had just been reading Dickens's *Christmas Carol*, and thought the offices of Scrooge and Marley probably looked something like this. I viewed a sojourn there with

111

extreme distaste, and was more than relieved to hear that their expected vacancy was not due for another two weeks or so. I secretly hoped that nothing more would come of it! We could do no more at this stage, so walked past Wilberforce House to Alfred Gelder Street, and then took a T/H tram home.

The ensuing few days were something of a hiatus. I paid a visit to the Public Library, did a few jobs about the house, had one or two walks through the park, but late February and early March were not the best times for outdoor activities. Then one evening, my sister spotted in the "situations vacant" section of the evening paper, an advertisement for an office boy required by a firm of shipbrokers, Armstrong, Lord & Co., with offices at 52, King Edward Street, Hull. Why not try for this, and see what the outcome was? There was always the chance that I might have to wait for weeks or months before the next Wilson Line vacancy. So without more ado, I wrote out an application and posted it. We had been having instruction at school on how to set out a letter of application to prospective employers, and I modelled it on these lines.

Three or four days later, I received a letter asking me to attend at their offices for an interview. 52, King Edward Street was a four-storey office block with the high sounding title of Ariel Chambers. It was of fairly recent construction, as indeed was most of King Edward Street, which as I mentioned earlier, had replaced a network of little old alleys eleven or twelve years previously. Ariel Chambers had a lift, rather unusual for 1917, and I found that Armstrong, Lord & Co., occupied the top floor, with one department (dealing with coal exporting) on the floor below.

I was determined to see this thing through on my own — I had not been too happy having my mother with me on the earlier occasion. It had savoured somewhat of "apron strings" although on the other hand it had served to break the ice as far as interviews were concerned, and I was grateful for her backing. I felt, though, that the time had come for me to stand on my own feet. I didn't know much about lifts and how to use them, so walked up the numerous flights of stairs until I reached the top floor, when I had a feeling of uneasiness and apprehension. I was wearing a clean Eton collar and my best jersey, and had given my boots an extra polish before leaving home. After a moment's pause to take a deep breath, I rang the bell in the enquiry lobby. A sliding panel opened, and the face of a youth appeared whom I took to be about fifteen years of age. I explained my errand, and a minute or two later I was ushered into a nicely carpeted office to meet Mr. Elder, the manager, who had signed the letter in answer to my application.

Mr. Elder asked a number of questions, including why I had left school at the age of thirteen, and was I interested in ships and shipping. I answered him as best I could, and showed him my school reference. A man of about forty, clean shaven, he spoke in a rather quick, decisive tone, and said that if

112

I was chosen for the vacancy, my main tasks would be, initially, delivering messages around the town and dock area, and attending to the outgoing mail. The interview was soon over, and I was told that I would be notified if I was successful — there were other applicants.

I walked down the many flights of stairs again, up King Edward Street, past the Wilberforce Monument, and crossed the bridge — Monument Bridge — before turning along Queen's Dockside. I lingered here for a while, watching the shipping, coasters, keels, the odd sailing schooner, and one or two tugs. There was a strong smell of tarry rope, mingling with the scent of alcohol coming from the nearby bonded warehouse where casks of wine and brandy awaited clearance and removal. I wondered if, soon, this world of shipping which hitherto I had seen only as a spectator, would embrace me in its arms. The prospect was an exciting one. With these thoughts in my mind, I caught a tram home — the fare was only ½d for children all the way from the City Square to the Aberdeen Street terminus.

During this period before getting a job, I had got into the lazy habit of staying in bed while the morning rush of getting ready for work and school by Dorothy and Dennis was in progress. Then, a few days later, when I was wondering if I ought to be bestirring myself, my mother called from the hall, "Bernie, the post's a bit late this morning, but there's a letter for you." I jumped out of bed and ran downstairs; this would be about 9 o'clock. Opening the envelope, this was what I read:

Hull, March 13th, 1917.

Dear Sir,

With reference to your application of the 8th inst., and your interview with us, we should be glad if you would kindly take up your duties tomorrow morning.

Your commencing salary will be 22/6d. per month. Should you adapt yourself quickly to the work entrusted to you, we shall grant you an increase on the 1st July.

Our office hours are — 9 a.m. to 6 p.m. with 1½ hours for lunch.

Yours faithfully,

Per pro Armstrong, Lord & Co.

W. H. Elder.

I gasped! Then re-read the letter to let the details sink in. "Take up your duties tomorrow morning....." Why, that was today, and it was already after 9 o'clock and I wasn't even dressed! As I hadn't turned up, would they have already written me off, and be on the point of writing to someone else? Mother said, "Be quick and get dressed, there's no time for any breakfast, but I'll get you a cup of cocoa and you can take a sandwich with you. You'll have to apologise, and tell them the post didn't arrive until 9 o'clock."

I hastily dressed, and while I was gulping down the cup of cocoa, my mother ran her eye over me to see if my parting was straight and face

113

reasonably clean. Then I ran up the street, and was lucky to catch a tram just arriving at the Lee Street stop. How slowly that wretched tram seemed to trundle along. Then, when we arrived at North Bridge, the bridge was "up" to let a string of barges through — more minutes lost while I sat and fumed. At last we arrived at "Bank" corner in George Street, and I nipped past the Andrew Marvell monument, down Jameson Street to Ariel Chambers, racing up the many flights of stairs two at a time.

Entering the enquiry lobby, I paused for a minute to get my breath and then rang the bell with some trepidation. The same cheeky looking 15-year-old answered the bell, and then took me to Mr. Elder's room where a knock on the door brought the response, "Come in." I told him how the post hadn't arrived until 9 o'clock, and I had come as quickly as possible. "That's all right," he said, "I know we didn't give you much notice." He introduced me to Mr. Greig, his assistant, who looked after the coal exporting side of the firm's business, and then took me into the general office where three or four clerks were sitting at their desks.

A Mr. Lonsdale was in charge of the office, and the postal desk was in a corner near one of the windows which looked down on King Edward Street, many feet below. It appeared that George, the 15-year-old, and an older colleague were to initiate me into the intricacies of the mailing system, and I was told to hold myself in readiness for any errands, or messages / documents which required delivery around the town area. Lunch intervals were spelled, and mine was to be from 1 to 2.30. The general office was bright and airy, very different from the gloomy High Street premises I had recently been in for interview, and which I found later was typical of office accommodation in that part of the city. The morning passed very quickly, and allowing about twenty-five minutes each way for travelling, I had ample time to get home for my lunch break. Obviously, I had quite a story to tell my mother when I arrived, and she seemed relieved that events had panned out so well.

The office staff turned out to be quite friendly, and I was to get to know them better as time went on. With the wartime demand for manpower for the forces, it was natural that industry and commerce should draw on women, and munition factories as well as offices were recruiting female workers, Armstrong, Lord & Co. being no exeption to the general rule. Apart from the two lady typists, there was a female cashier, a woman in her mid-thirties who was a ledger clerk, and a pretty girl of about eighteen who was the telephonist. The males were the manager and his assistant, the elderly Mr. Lonsdale, two young Customs Clerks — one about to be called up — and two juniors. One of the juniors was about to be promoted to Customs Clerk, hence the vacancy for another junior which I was filling.

I soon learned that the "girls" had an afternoon break for a cup of tea and a nibble, and I, as the newest arrival, was expected to slip along to a nearby confectioners for whipped cream walnuts which the ladies relished with their

114

cup of tea. My reward as an occasional sample of these delicacies ("get one for yourself, Bernard"), so I was never reluctant to be sent out on this errand! During lunch intervals and tea breaks, the office juniors had to man the switchboard, and I was initiated by Miss Sizer into the mysteries of making trunk calls, holding on, switching through, and disconnecting extensions after calls. In a shipping office, the telephone was constantly in use, as apart from Customs formalities, exchange of information with shippers on discharge and loading information, ships' master's personal calls, etc., each vessel had to be supplied with food and supplies, from tinned goods and sides of bacon to tarpaulin and towels. As periods in port were extremely limited, all such work had to be negotiated at speed, and the telephone was a vital part of the proceedings.

The mailing duties consisted of writing out the necessary envelopes, folding and inserting the various letters and documents, licking and putting on the postage stamps (there were no sponge pads), sealing and entering all the completed letters under names of recipients in the stamp ledger, and finally posting the mail at King Edward Street Post Office, just round the corner. Although the official office hours finished at 6 p.m., we were quite frequently receiving mail on the postal desk in quantity up to shortly before that time, which meant that the office juniors seldom got away before 6.30. We were expected to balance the stamp ledger with receipts and usages before leaving the office, but sometimes put this off until the next morning, which, however, meant getting in early, as the ledger and stamp stocks had to be handed in to the cashier shortly after 9 o'clock for checking stocks with ledger. If crafty George couldn't balance, it was a simple matter to put in a few fictitious entries, and no-one was the wiser!

If by any chance we missed the 7 p.m. collection from King Edward Street, we had to trek to the G.P.O. in the Old Town, where night mail closed an hour later. As this was not too far off my route home — the T/H trams serving Holderness passed that way — it usually fell to my lot to take mail to the Head Post Office when necessary.

The last day of the month was the office pay day, when the cashier brought round our pay packets. My £1.2.6d per month worked out at just over 5/- a week, not a princely sum by any means, even for those days, but it was a welcome addition to the family finances. It was augmented occasionally by a meal allowance of 1/-. This was paid if we worked after 7 p.m., or if through delivering urgent messages or documents in the city or dock area, our lunch break was disrupted. When my lunch hour was so interrupted, I used to go to Jefferson's vegetarian food stores in Savile Street, where they sold bean and tomato pies costing only 2d. These pies filled with butter beans, onions and tomato, were very tasty, and kept me going until teatime. My favourite haunt for eating, weather permitting, was one of the seats on the promenade top of the Corporation Pier, from where one had a panoramic view of the

115

Humber and its shipping. I quite welcomed these breaks, for not only did I have an outing to the Pier, but made a profit of 10d on the deal, or 9d if I treated myself to a bottle of lemonade or a cup of tea from a market stall.

One of the features of the Corporation Pier and its approaches at the time of which I am writing, was the Horse Wash or 'Oss Wash as it was colloquially known. This was an incline built of stone setts leading down from the roadway to the inner basin which at low water is just an area of mud. From half tide to high water, however, the water rises until the steps disappear below water level, and in the days of horse-drawn transport this provided an easy method for carters to unhitch their dusty animals and give them a well-earned dip! It was a common occurrence to see the horses enjoying their ablutions, as they waded into the water.

A week or two after I started work, Grandma Heald died at South Ferriby, shortly before the end of March. Her illness, which had already started when I was on holiday at her house in the previous August, had been diagnosed as cancer. I had looked on her as quite an old lady, but she was only 73, and perhaps it was her cloak and Victorian bonnet which she wore when dressed to go out, that made her look older than she was. Her passing

The Horse Wash ('Oss Wash), Hull Corporation Pier, about 1910.

116

left quite a gap, and South Ferriby was never quite the same afterwards, for to me she epitomised more than anyone else the family traditions and rural background of earlier generations.

The war news in the first half of 1917 was far from inspiring. The Germans had started their ruthless U-Boat campaign, and were sinking every ship they could locate, neutral or belligerent, in the European sea approaches. Unchecked, this could have brought us to our knees, but three things helped to counter the situation. These were (1) rationing of foods, (2) the introduction of the convoy system at sea and (3) a massive programme of shipbuilding. One of the results of rationing was the introduction of war-time flour containing a large percentage of potato. This flour had a dark texture, and the loaves made from it had a dark grey appearance. Another effect of the shortages was the almost total disappearance of imported tinned foods, while butter, meat and sugar had to be used very sparingly.

Our garden at home was too small to join in the "Dig for Victory" campaign which had developed to counteract the food shortage. The use of allotments on suitable spare ground was encouraged by the Government, and vegetable plots sprang into existence almost overnight. Prior to 1917, vegetable allotments in suburban areas were almost unknown. Our own effort in the provision of food was to build a small chicken run with a covered nesting place. Our milkman, whose premises were a farmhouse with outbuildings (long since pulled down), adjacent to the present Crown Inn on Holderness Road, supplied us with four pullets. These were a White Leghorn, a White Leghorn/Wyandotte cross, a Brown Leghorn and a Plymouth Rock. We named these pullets Biddy, Cheeky, Brownie, and Speckle. The first three were prolific layers right from the start, but Speckle was constantly broody, and never achieved her hoped-for potential. Dorothy kept a record of layings, and in the first year, Biddy, Cheeky and Brownie each exceeded 200 eggs, more than paying for their keep, and making us self-sufficient in eggs. This reminds me of a story I heard about the teacher who was telling his class about hens and their egg laying, in a biology lesson. "The average hen," he said, "lays about 600 eggs in its lifetime. What do we do with her after that?" One bright youth, whose father was in the trade, replied, "Cut off 'er head, and sell 'er for a spring chicken."

The clatter and clang of the riveters' tools was heard night and day at Earle's Yard on Hedon Road, as ships grew on their stocks. At home, we had a bout of the "might have beens" as we thought of the lost possibilities of our erstwhile shipyard at Ferriby Sluice, and the thumping order books which would have ensued if the yard — and Dad — had survived to the war years. What a difference this would have made to our fortunes. We had occasional visits from our cousins, Stanley and Arthur Heald. Stanley, as mentioned earlier, had been in the Territorials before the war and was serving in the Royal Artillery, while Arthur, who had gone through the Trinity House

117

School for nautical training, was now a third officer with the Prince Line, trading mainly with the West Indies and Central America. Their widowed mother, Grace Heald, had been schoolmistress at Garton-in-Holderness for some years, and was now in charge of the village school at Ellerby between Hull and Hornsea. She, too, occasionally cycled into Hull and called in on us to tell us the latest news of her sons, the youngest of whom, Norman, was almost due for calling up.

One gleam of sunshine in the generally disturbing war news was the entry of the United States of America on the allied side in April 1917. Goaded beyond bearing by the ruthless submarine which was costing American lives, the patience of President Wilson and the American nation was finally exhausted, and the mighty potential of the U.S.A. was a welcome addition to the allied strength. This was later to be partially balanced by the defection of Russia and her withdrawal from the war through the Revolution of November 1917, when the moderate Kerenski was soon swept away, and a Communist state brought into the power, which left Germany free to concentrate all her forces in the west.

CHAPTER EIGHTEEN

I had now settled in happily at the shipping office, and had no wish to make a change in the immediate future, so I wrote a letter to Thomas Wilson's asking to be removed from their waiting list, as I had obtained suitable alternative employment. I have often wondered what would have happened if I had transferred to them, for not long after the war there was a shipping slump and the Wilson Line was taken over by the Ellerman group, and the fleet became Ellerman's Wilson Line. The slump brought about massive unemployment in the shipping world, and I might well have joined the ranks of the unemployed. By then, however, I had became part of a new and exciting industry, of which more later.

In spite of the hard work which the job entailed, we in the office, and especially the juniors, had our interludes of fun. It was not long before George showed me a weakness in the apparatus which worked the lift. The building, as I have mentioned, had four floors — and a basement — and a resident caretaker had rooms at the back of the building on the ground floor.

Comings and goings at the various offices meant that the lift was in fairly frequent use. It was self-operated, and when the outer gate was closed, completing the circuit, one pressed the button for the requisite floor. However, as demonstrated by George, if one released the catch on any of the gates while the lift was in operation, the lift stopped dead in its tracks.

At one stage, a minor feud had broken out between us and a belligerent office boy employed on another floor, and this had developed into a sparring contest. Even I, who was normally of a placid disposition, exchanged jeers, and had my nose punched once or twice. George's idea of retribution was to wait discreetly out of sight until our friend was in the lift, and then stop him between floors.

The opportunity soon arrived. I watched him from a landing corner get in and start the lift, and then signalled to George on the floor above. He quickly released the catch, and the lift stopped with a jerk. Looking down, we could hear muffled sounds of annoyance, the lift shook, he rattled the gate, but of course nothing happened. A few minutes later, while we were thoroughly enjoying the little drama, someone below opened an office door, saw the lift stuck, and a shouting conversation took place. Then the newcomer walked down the staircase to the ground floor and called the caretaker. Meanwhile, George and I, peering down, could hardly contain ourselves. Eventually the caretaker arrived, and at this point George silently closed the third floor gate. The caretaker pressed the ground floor button, and immediately the lift was on the move again.

Now we slipped back quickly into the office to start addressing envelopes assiduously, and tried to imagine what was happening between caretaker and boy. We hoped it was something like this: "What a dolt you are — it only needed firm pressure on the button. How long is it since you left the Infants School?" "But I pushed and pushed the button, it just wouldn't work." "Of course it would. Now look here, I'm a busy man, and don't like being interrupted, so if you can't work the lift you'd better start walking." Needless to say, this prank was a potentially dangerous one, and dearly though we would have liked to repeat it, we decided that if we were found out, the consequences might be rather unpleasant — but we'd won that round! So it wasn't attempted again, by us at any rate.

One other escapade comes to my mind. Again, George was the instigator. It was one day when most of the staff were away at lunch, that we made our way to an alcove at the back of the top floor where a window opened out on to a ledge with a low parapet. Climbing through this window, we dropped on to the ledge, walked a few feet, and then jumped a gap on to the next roof section. Had we slipped and fallen, the concreted area was a good fifty feet below, and that would have been the end of us. However, we were safely across, and dropped on to the domed roof of what was then the Rudge-Whitworth building at the corner of King Edward Street and Waltham Street. Here, there was a parapet about three feet high, behind which we were reasonably safe.

What a lovely bird's eye view we had of the scene below! The trams were far below us, and we had conquered our Everest! One or two pedestrians looking upwards spotted us, and then more and more, so we waved and blew kisses to them. Suddenly we realised that if we were caught up there, we should be in for trouble. So, our momentary triumph over, we hastily retraced our steps round the dome, walked along the ledge to our open window, and heaved ourselves through. A quick wash in the lavatory, and we were back at our mailing desk, respectable citizens once more.

Fortunately, there were no repercussions, and if there had been any enquiries as to what two boys had been doing on the roof of a prominent business house, they must soon have been dropped. I think we realised on reflection that this had been a dangerous exploit, so we kept quiet about it and never attempted it again.

One feature of our office equipment, which has long disappeared with the march of time, was a speaking tube between the general office and the floor below housing the coal exporting office with the assistant manager and his shorthand typist. This tube was used in conjunction with a lift about eighteen inches square worked by a rope and pulley which was used for hauling up and down stationery, small goods items, tea trays, etc. It was also used when signed typewritten letters from below were ready for the postal desk, and saved quite a lot of running up and down stairs.

When communication was required, one blew into the tube and this actuated a high pitched whistle at the other end. Putting the tube to one's ear, one would hear the answerer call, "Yes, what is it?" or something similar, and a reasonably lucid conversation would ensue, followed by the using of the lift tray. I remember one of the customs clerks who had had some slight difference of opinion with the typist down below, blowing a raspberry through to her when she answered the whistle, the response being that she threatened to report him to her boss if it happened again!

The customs clerks had something of a roving commission, for not only had they to meet the captains of the ships when they arrived in port, acting as mentors and guides, but they had to arrange clearances at the Custom House, facilitate any business with Trinity House, and arrange pilotage, tugs, etc., for outgoing vessels.

For my part, I became very familiar with the ramifications of the shipping interests in the port. Frequent visits were made to the Custom House in Lowgate for the approval and stamping of Shipping Bills. I used to scan the notice boards in the vestibule there which were full of "notices to mariners," with details of any obstructions on the river, movements of buoys, non-operation of lights, etc. One poster which always caught my eye was a prominent one displaying a huge illustration of a Colorado beetle with its tell-tale stripes, and a warning of the need to notify the health authorities if any of these destructive creatures were observed in cargo or elsewhere. All sorts of strange animals could sometimes appear in tropical cargoes, particularly fruit, from scorpions to snakes. One of the clerks had a matchbox containing a spider — dead of course — found in a cargo of bananas. It was the biggest spider I have ever seen, and just fitted inside the box.

I used to take cheques for the payment of wharfage accounts to the Dock Offices near Monument Bridge, to the Tug Company for towage, and to the Pilot Offices near the Pier for the payment of pilotage dues. Sometimes my business took me to the legal and insurance quarter in Land of Green Ginger, Bowlalley Lane and High Street. I got to know a number of short cuts from thoroughfare to thoroughfare — for instance one could slip through the corridors of a block of offices from Silver Street to Bowlalley Lane without using the streets themselves.

Flanking Market Place and Mytongate were a number of alleys and side streets like Dagger Lane, Robinson Row, Fetter Lane and Finkle Street where one seemed to bridge the centuries to earlier times, and might almost expect to see the ghosts of the press gangs and their captives. Of the old buildings still standing, Ye Olde White Harte Hotel in Silver Street is known locally for its "plotting room" where Sir John Hotham and his council decided to close the gates of the town to King Charles I in 1642, a decision which was to spark off the Civil War.

I have already mentioned Sir William De la Pole, who was knighted by Edward I and became the town's first mayor in 1299. The family prospered for over 200 years and the title of Earl of Suffolk was bestowed on one of their number. They married into royalty, and in the time of Edward IV were very close in succession to the throne. A statue of Sir William stands near the Corporation Pier and he is seen gazing into the city from the edge of the broad estuary which brought fame and fortune to his family.

I was always very pleased when I was required to visit ships in dock to take or collect documents such as ships' manifests, or bills of lading. The smell of tarry rope, engine oil and steam was like ambrosia, and the climbing of gangways and steel ladders was exercise for the gods! If I could get on to the bridge, so much the better. Most of the captains with whom I came in contact were very understanding, and if one showed interest in their ship they were usually happy to detail one of the crew to show a wide-eyed youngster around.

One captain, whom I remember well, was the master of the *Bay Fisher*, a stocky, genial man of about fifty. He was generous to a degree, and I never came away from his ship without receiving a shilling tip. I once had to take some documents to his vessel when dusk was closing in on a late November afternoon. When I arrived at Humber Dock where *Bay Fisher* had been loading cargo, I found she had left the quayside, and was moored to a buoy in the middle of the dock — she was due to sail on the next tide. Here was a pickle. How was I to get on board? I thought for a moment, and then shouted as loud as I could, "*Bay Fisher*, ahoy!" A voice called back, "What is it?" "Documents for the captain," I replied. A few minutes later, I saw someone climb over the side into the ship's dinghy, which was secured by a rope, cast off, and scull towards where I was standing by a flight of stone steps on the dock side. Approaching the steps, the seaman called out, "Jump in," and from the bottom step I leapt in.

What a thrill to be rowed into the middle of the dock in the semi-darkness, with the ship's dim lights making a pattern on the water. Reaching the vessel, I climbed up the rope ladder, heaved myself over the ship's rail and went to the captain's cabin. As I handed the envelope over and waited for the captain's written acknowledgement, he gave me a quizzical look and said, "Well, son, if you'd been an hour later, we should have been out in the river, and might have had to take you to Spain with us. How would you have liked that?" Thinking of the possibilities of mines and German submarines, I replied, "If the war was over, I should have liked it very much, sir, but my mother would have been very worried if I'd gone with you now." There seemed little more to say, and with a pat on the back and "Good lad," the captain gave me the usual tip. Then I was sitting in the dinghy again, and being propelled across the quay-side. As the water lapped the gunwale, and the pattern of light made kaleidoscopic designs on the surface of the tide, I wondered if it felt something like this to be on the Grand Canal at Venice, propelled by a gondolier. Sadly, some time later, I heard that the *Bay Fisher* had been lost with all hands.

Albert Dock, Hull, 1905-6.

Having started my job with the shipping agents as recently as March, I was only entitled to a week's holiday that year, which again was spent at South Ferriby in August — this time with our second cousins, the Milners. Harvesting was in progress, but Fred Milner, now 19, was in the army, and with Grandma Heald gone, the old carefree days seemed to have departed, but I did enjoy the farmhouse fare including lots of bacon and eggs.

One incident I remember vividly, happened when I was standing in an elevated cornfield with a panoramic view across the Humber of North Ferriby and the swelling skyline of the Yorkshire Wolds. In brilliant sunshine, I watched a thunder shower slowly moving down the estuary on the Yorkshire side. The inky blackness of the thunder-cloud was accentuated by the brilliance on the southern side of the river. Through the curtains of rain, blotting out the details of the farther shore, forked lightning flickered and sparkled over the woodland and water like a celestial firework display.

From where I stood, the sound of the thunder was muted by distance, but the whole scene was like some apocalyptic relevation of divine authority, and I a spell-bound spectator of the infinite wonder. It was the first time I had seen such an exhibition, and the majesty of it remains with me still. I have sometimes wondered if St. John had witnessed something like this on the island of Patmos, which could have sparked off his "Revelation of St. John the Divine."

In the September of that year, the last of my grandparents, Granpa Hollingworth, died at the age of 75. As I was thirteen years old, my mother thought I ought to attend the funeral, which was early one mid-week afternoon. This, of course, entailed asking for time off. In those days it was a standard joke that when office boys wanted time off to attend an important cricket or football match, or other good reason known to themselves, they asked for leave of absence "to attend my grandfather's funeral." Now, here was I faced with the real thing, a state of affairs which was not at all to my liking. Would I be refused, or asked for proof, or worst of all, asked where the important match was being played? I needn't have worried, though. When I knocked on Mr. Elder's door and entered, wearing a worried if not guilty look, as well as my black tie, and put my request, he just said, "Of course, boy, get back as soon as you can afterwards."

Through his set expression, I thought I detected just a ghost of something which might have developed into a smile after I had gone. I remember very little about the funeral. It certainly hadn't the impact of my father's death five years previously. There were the usual coaches drawn by black horses, and near relatives, with Uncle Joe Hollingworth on special leave in his blue "wounded" uniform, but the details are quite blurred.

Evening classes started in September, and it had been arranged that I should attend the Craven Street Continuation Centre, to study commercial geography and shorthand. It was considered that being in a shipping office,

124

an extension of my geographical knowledge and the ability when answering the phone to take down messages in shorthand would be an asset. I found, as I expected, the geography lessons interesting. We learned quite a lot about the textile industry, the iron and steel trade, mining and exporting of coal among other things. With the coal exporting side of Armstrong, Lord's shipping business and the information received at the evening classes in mind, the names on the sides of the railway wagons seen rattling over the level crossings took on reality. Hickleton, Brodsworth, Manvers Main, Cortonwood Wath, and Shirebrook not only meant something, but I could picture their places of origin and the processes which had led to their cargoes of coal arriving in Hull.

Coal hoists were a feature of the Hull docks in those days when oil fuel for ships' bunkering was in its infancy. The rattle and roar as the coal wagons released their loads down the chutes into the ships' holds or bunkers was almost as familiar a sound as the tooting of tugs and the deeper notes of the ocean-going steamers changing berths or preparing to sail.

I found the shorthand class, where the Pitman system was being taught, a complete contrast. I remembered the Rt. Hon. T. R. Ferens M.P., head of Reckitts and superintendent at Brunswick Wesleyan Sunday School (which I still attended in spite of earlier mentioned traumatic experiences), saying that it was the learning of shorthand which had first put him on the road to his highly successful commercial career, as a young man in the 1860's. Hopefully, I was soon being initiated into the mysteries of thick and thin lines, curves and dots, and repeating pee, bee; tee, dee; eff, vee; ith, thee; chay, jay; etc.

Unfortunately however, our teacher had difficulty in keeping discipline. He was a slightly-built man with a club foot, and easy game for some of the "students" who obviously had no interest in learning, and were only there for a lark — and the girls. Most of the brighter pupils had earlier been creamed off to the secondary and grammar schools, and I suppose the less intelligent and undisciplined ones set the pace here. At any rate, with the amount of tomfoolery going on, interruptions, etc., it was difficult to learn, and I felt sorry for our teacher trying to pass on his knowledge, but with no idea how to control the disruptive element. At the end of the session, I had managed to write shorthand at the rate of 50 words a minute — just enough for a pass — and in the circumstances not too bad a result, I thought.

It was about this time that brother Dennis went down with scarlet fever. This normally meant the victims going to the isolation hospital off the Wawne Road, near Sutton, colloquially known as the "Fever Hospital," and we had from time to time seen juvenile patients taken away from their homes in the yellow "Fever" cab, with other youngsters gazing at the sight with a morbid interest, and wondering when it would be their turn.

However, mother undertook to keep Dennis isolated at home, and this was achieved by confining him alone in the back bedroom (which he and I normally shared) and draping a blanket soaked in disinfectant over the door. During the period of isolation, three or four weeks, I slept in the front bedroom occupied by my mother and sister. This was a big room and decorum was observed by putting a screen across the portion of the room where I slept. Thanks to the isolation and my mother's careful routine, no-one else caught the infection, and it was a great day when the authorities came to fumigate the back bedroom.

After having measles and mumps as a small child, the only illnesses I seem to have contracted were a bout of dysentry, the origin of which was never discovered, and jaundice, a liver condition in which the complexion goes extremely yellow. During this latter complaint I had to be kept off all savouries, and was restricted to a bland diet of milk, rice pudding, etc. I well remember the relish of being able to enjoy once again, after the illness had passed, roast beef and particularly dumplings swimming in gravy!

CHAPTER NINETEEN

The winter of 1917-18, during which I had my fourteenth birthday, came and went. The dreadful stalemate on the Western Front, and the horrors of Paschendaele with its terrible slaughter, were succeeded by the hammer blows of the German offensive in March 1918, when all the small gains of territory won after years of fighting and enormous casualties were swept away in the great advance of Ludendorff which drove the Allies back almost to the gates of Paris. With no Eastern Front to man, all the German strength could be exerted in the West. Gradually the advance was halted, but for several anxious months the issue of the war was in the balance.

Meanwhile, at home, work went on as usual. A few spasmodic Zeppelin raids took place, but most of the nights of air raid warnings passed off without incident. On one occasion, however, a Zeppelin did breach the coastal defences, but by now we were getting a bit blasé, and made no attempt to take cover when the air raid buzzers sounded. After perhaps an hour, we heard gunfire, and this was the signal to tumble out of bed and go downstairs. Mother lit a candle, and as the sound of anti-aircraft gunfire got rapidly louder, we all crouched under the big living room table. Just then, we heard a rushing sound rather like the approach of a hissing express train, and this increased in intensity until there was a thud, the ground shook, and the candle jumped off the floor and settled again.

For a few minutes we crouched, terrified, until the gunfire gradually subsided and silence reigned again. After a while, I went outside and groups of people were collecting, full of theories as to what had been happening. Eventually the All Clear sounded, but we had to wait until the next day before the truth of the incident was revealed. The rushing sound was the noise of a big aerial torpedo being dropped from the raider, the first of its kind to be experienced in the Hull area. It had fortunately landed on agricultural ground where now the Bilton Grange Estate stands, then, of course, still undeveloped. At the first available opportunity I went to have a look at the crater, and was astonished at its size. It would easily have held two tramcars, and was a big hole, even by later 1939-45 standards. The missile which caused it must have been quite the most powerful of the war as far as Hull was concerned.

Among the features which tended to lighten the sober and rather fatalist atmosphere on the home front, two in particular deserve mention. One was Charlie Chaplin's films — his *Shoulder Arms* with its parody of life at the front caused many a laugh to cinema-goers, and the scene where Charlie lies floating in a flooded dugout with his head and feet showing above the water level, and the inimitable bland expression, must have brought a smile to many viewers, and released them for a while from the anxieties of war. The other was Bruce Bairnfather's *Old Bill* cartoons which first appeared in the

127

Bystander. These again looked at the lighter side of the conflict, and Old Bill, the British "Tommy" with the walrus moustache, became a national figure. Probably two of the best ones were "If you know of a better 'ole, go to it," with Bill and his mate arguing by a flooded shell hole, and "What time do they feed the sea-lions, Alf?" with Bill and his walrus moustache hardly distinguishable from the real creatures at the zoo.

At the office, the routine was much as it had been when I started work over twelve months previously. One source of comparative discontent was that I rarely arrived home before 7 p.m., and with evening classes beginning at 7.30 this meant little or no tea before I had to be out again on class nights. Most city offices were closing at 5.30, but with ours being nominally 6 o'clock, and the mail to be handled and posted after that, we seemed to be working long after everybody else had gone home. In addition, salaries were low, and although I was now getting £2 per calendar month, this represented little more than 9/- per week.

I was at this unsettled stage, when I heard that a vacancy for a junior was about to occur at the Shell Oil Installation at Salt End, owing to one of their staff being called up for military service. Salt End is an area on the river frontage east of King George Dock, then owned by the North Eastern Railway Company, who had seen its commercial possibilities. Shortly before the war, they had built an oil jetty 1500 feet in length, reaching out over the mudflats into deep water, and had leaseed land for development to various oil concerns. By August, 1914, three had built terminals and storage tanks and had started operations. These were the Asiatic Petroleum Company, the Anglo-Mexican Petroleum Products Company, and the Yorkshire Oil Storage Company. A fourth, the Anglo-American Oil Company (later to be known as Esso), who already had a small installation up-river at West Dock Street near Sir William Wright Dock, had secured a site but had erected only one tank when war broke out and suspended operations. Yet another oil company, British Petroleum, who had a depot at Dairycoates, were to move to Salt End in 1921.

The Asiatic Petroleum Company, whose main sources of oil were the Dutch East Indies, notably Borneo and Sumatra, had arranged for their products to be marketed in this country by their associates, the Shell concern, and the "Shell" Marketing Company had just been formed for this purpose. It was at this stage that I applied for the vacancy of office junior, and after an interview was accepted for the post which to my delight carried a salary of 10/- per week plus 5/- war bonus, a big advance on my previous earnings, and it carried a promise of a career with one of the leading oil companies then at the beginning of a period of unprecedented expansion.

The office hours were 9 to 5.30 with an hour for lunch, and I started my new job on 21st May, 1918. In many respects I was sorry to leave my post with the shipping agents and their friendly staff, but I knew that my move

128

carried far better prospects. My reference read:

"We have pleasure in certifying that Thomas Bernard Heald has been in our employ as Office Boy from March 1917 until the present date. During that time he has given us entire satisfaction, and we can confidently recommend him to anyone requiring a conscientious steady worker. He leaves of his own accord to take up another position."

Per pro Armstrong, Lord & Co.

W. H. Elder.   18th May, 1918.

What a contrast travelling to work was in this new situation! Instead of the busy Holderness Road with its unpredictable traffic delays in the shape of the Southcoates level crossing and the North Bridge shipping, I now made for the open country on my bicycle after passing Marfleet Lane tram terminus. The route to Salt End lay along the road to Hedon, then just a country lane bordered by hawthorn hedges, at that season white with May blossom, and its intoxicating scent was a complete change from the smells of a city. Salt End Lane, where the way to the oil installations left the Hedon Road, was almost a bird reserve with tits, finches, blackbirds, willow and sedge warblers. At one point, a sedge warbler sang his jumbled chattering song morning after morning in exactly the same place, week after week.

My new manager, Mr. E. E. Boorman, and the chief clerk, Mr. Robinson, made me welcome, and I was initiated into my duties. At that time operational staff worked a 53-hour week, beginning at 6 a.m., with a breakfast break from 8 to 8.30, and a "dinner" interval from 12 to 1, the working day ending at 5 p.m. and 12 noon on Saturdays. Each operative had a numbered disc which he took from a similarly numbered hook, on starting work, and dropped into a strong wooden box furnished with a lock.

Five minutes after starting time, the box was removed by the gateman, and any workman arriving after that time lost a "quarter" or two hours pay. One of my jobs was to enter the various numbered discs into a time book against corresponding names, and from this record the weekly hours were assessed by the wages clerk. It was not until some time later than a modern system with clocks and time cards was introduced. One routine practice which intrigued me greatly was the ringing by the gatemen of a handbell (which had developed a crack!) to mark starting and leaving times and break periods.

The period of which I am writing was several years before the invention by Bowser (who incidentally married a cousin of mine) of the kerbside pump which bears his name. It was a great leap forward when, around 1924, "Bowsers" began to come into operation, revolutionising the distribution of motor spirit to garages, and its subsequent sale direct into the customers' tanks. In 1918 movements of motor spirit were of necessity in either cans or barrels, and the only bulk road tankers coming in and out of Salt End were

129

two horse-drawn vehicles engaged in delivering S.B.P., or Special Boiling Point spirit, to the oil mills at Wilmington and Stoneferry. Here, the British Extracting Company and H.O.M.Co. (The Hull Oil Manufacturing Company) used this special low gravity spirit when processing their raw materials into feed for cattle.

It seems strange, and a passage back in time, that when oil-well production is referred to in company reports or the press it is quoted in barrels rather than tons. Trade nomenclature dies hard! Deliveries to inland depots were in steel barrels, or more usually, cans and cases, loaded into rail wagons. In the case of the larger depots like Leeds and Sheffield, bulk tank wagons, or rail-cars as we called them, carrying about 2600 gallons, were used. Local deliveries were in the almost universal two-gallon cans packed into the very early solid-tyred motor lorries, or horse-drawn rullies which were still in use at that time.

One of my jobs was to take note of the day's rail deliveries, select appropriate addressed labels from alphabetically arranged piegon holes, and attach these to a special clip on the loaded tank car or wagon. I also took a record each morning of the numbered tank cars in the sidings which included new arrivals brought in empty by the previous shunt. In movements by rail, we worked in close conjunction with the railway staff at King George Dock, and their Salt End representative, as our rail sidings were an extension of the dock network.

I found a study of the buildings and apparatus which made up an oil installation profoundly interesting. Supplies, which were refined overseas, arrived by ocean tanker carrying up to about 16,000 tons. The oil companies had adopted specialised names for their tanker fleets, the Shell group, as befitted their title, choosing sea shells like *Patella* and *Donax*, while the Anglo-American Company, with their Latin-American connections, chose the names of saints, e.g. *San Lorenzo* and *San Pedro*.

Once the hoses were connected to the ships' tanks, the oil was pumped through pipelines along the 1500 feet of the river jetty to the pump-house manifold, and from there into the various storage tanks, the biggest of which at that time held about 3,000 tons, or rather less than a million gallons. A boiler-house supplied the steam power to work the pumps which distributed the oil to the storage tanks, and the fillers of railcars, barrels and cans, which were the next links in the delivery chain.

Rail-cars were filled from an overhead gantry through swing arms which entered the tank lid, and after all were filled, they were drawn by a steam capstan over a weighbridge which recorded the gross weight. The tare was painted on the vehicle, and the nett was the difference between the two. In the office, the nett weight was multiplied by the specific gravity to obtain the gallonage involved. The calculations were carried out with the aid of a Brunsviga calculator, a huge machine with a handle and

130

a sliding base, a museum piece by modern standards but quite effective.

Cans were filled from an overhead container by teams of youths under the supervision of a foreman. A battery of twenty or so freshly painted cans would be placed in position, with pipes leading down into their filler caps. A valve was opened, and two gallons of petrol, controlled through a gauge, would be poured into the cans. These were then fitted with a faucet cap and sealed with a wire-attached metal seal.

Under wartime regulations, company brands, i.e., B.P., Shell, and Pratts (later Esso) were not allowed, and standard quality "Pool" petrol was the only kind marketed for general use in the then universal khaki cans. There was one exception however, and this was where aviation spirit was concerned. From the outbreak of war until 1917, all petrol for the Royal Flying Corps was "Shell Aviation" in the familiar pre-war red cans, and the Company was allowed to continue this distinguishing colour.

Stringent precautions were taken to see that no foreign matter or contaminants could find its way into Aviation spirit and endanger the lives of pilots, and periodically we had a visit from a member of the Aeronautical Inspection Directorate who tested the filling equipment and took samples for analysis. This government department with its cumbersome title was always known as the A.I.D., and some years after the events recorded here, one of their officials told us of an embarrassing situation in which he was involved. When mentioning in mixed company that he was a member of the A.I.D., it was assumed that he was an artificial insemination donor, and aroused great interest among both sexes!

For assessing quantities in the storage tanks, a calibrated dipping line weighted at the end was used, each tenth of an inch representing perhaps a hundred gallons, depending of course on the size of the tank. Each tank was furnished with a vertical steel ladder up which the operative climbed before opening a lid and inserting the steel tape. This was a skilled job, as an error of a tenth of an inch either way made an appreciable difference.

It was no part of my job to climb tanks, but the lone tank on the unfinished Anglo-American site, easily reached through a gap in the fence, drew me like a magnet. So one day during the lunch interval I slipped under the corrugated iron fence, walked to the foot of the tank, gazed up the thirty feet of vertical ladder, and started to climb. I reached the top, hauled myself on to the tank roof and sat there for a while, admiring the view up-river to the long line of Hull docks. Then came reality! I came back to earth — figuratively — when I looked over the edge and down the vertical rungs. I panicked, and came out in a cold sweat as I realised that to reach safety I had to swing myself over the abyss and negotiate that awful ladder.

For a few minutes I lay back on the tank roof not daring to move, for a fall on to the concrete apron below would almost certainly prove fatal. Then, "You've got to do it," I told myself, "Tank dippers are running up and down

131

vertical ladders every day of their working lives." Eventually, I took a grip on myself, got a firm hold on the projecting hand-rail, and carefully felt for the topmost rungs with my feet. Then with heart beating furiously I started the descent, slowly, so slowly, but realising that every new foothold was a step nearer safety. At length I reached the ground, and breathed a deep sigh of relief. As might be expected, I kept the story of this exploit to myself, as I knew that if I had fallen in this deserted compound my body might have lain there for weeks without discovery. Although later on, I climbed tanks legitimately, it was with unease, and I still have an abhorrence of vertical heights. Some years later, it became standard pratice to furnish petroleum tanks with spiral ladders more like staircases, a much safer proposition.

In 1918 we had no canteen, but the workmen had a messroom with facilities for making tea. The office staff used a store room in the office building for eating, and sandwiches were the usual fare, although I sometimes went one better, and brought along one of my mother's home-made meat pies, which was hotted up in the men's messroom. Looking back over the years, it was a curious situation, to be in at the beginning of a great modern industry, yet in rather primitive conditions and in a largely rural area. The port of Hull was away to the west of us, Hedon with its tall church tower, "The King of Holderness," was $2\frac{1}{2}$ miles away by road, and the nearest inhabited area apart from two houses attached to the oil installation, was the Humberside village of Paull on the eastern side of the tidal Hedon Haven. By road, this was a roundabout five miles away, but a rickety footbridge had recently been thrown over the Haven for the passage of troops attached to the Paull anti-aircraft battery, and this brought the village within one mile by shank's pony, or bicycle.

Our telephone was a wall type, manually operated, and attached to the small Hedon exchange. Our telephone number (a single line only) was Hedon 20, and to make a call one turned the handle which rang a bell or dropped an indicator in the Hedon exchange, and was answered by the one operator, a lady, with whom we could have the occasional chat while asking her to get us the number required. It was a free and easy arrangement, far removed from the slick efficiency of today's S.T.D. Carbon copies of typewritten letters had just been introduced, replacing the cumbersome press which still stood in a place of honour, like some Dickensian relic from Scrooge's counting house.

The Royal Air Force had come into being on 1st April 1918, from the Royal Flying Corps and the Royal Naval Air Service, controlled by the Army and Navy authorities respectively. The R.A.F. was now an independent command, and new training stations were coming into operation at sites where landing strips could be conveniently used. Three of these, locally, were at Driffield, Hornsea and Withernsea, and we had regular visits from R.A.F. transport lorries which filled up with the red

Aviation Spirit cans. We also supplied motor spirit in the khaki cans to the R.A.S.C., and these big vehicles, mostly Albion and Thorneycrofts, without windscreens, were welcome visitors. Seeing them, one felt one was really in the war effort. This was underlined, when, during my first month, a lone hit-and-run Zeppelin slipped up the Humber and dropped a stick of bombs on the mudflats near the oil jetty, fortunately missing anything valuable.

About this time, my sister received from her employers an unexpected wage bonus, and as my 15/- per week had eased our financial difficulties, we decided to celebrate by having a holiday at Withernsea during late July. We obtained lodgings near the sea front for a fortnight, but I could only take a week in view of my short service. For the second week, I slept with the rest of the family at Withernsea, and cycled to Salt End each day. This entailed a fifteen mile journey night and morning, but the weather was good, and setting off from the coast about 7.30, I had an enjoyable journey in the freshness of the morning. I usually arrived back for my evening meal about 6.30 with the added bonus of an evening at the seaside and the chance of a dip. On my way out of, or into, Withernsea via England's Hill on the Hull road, I passed the newly established R.A.F. airfield, and it was a great thrill to see the Sopwiths and D.H.9's taking off and coming in to land, and realising that in a small way I had a hand in their exploits.

As there was no public transport between the oil terminal and the Hull Corporation tram terminus at Marfleet, the company had engaged a contractor who owned a covered wagonette, drawn by two horses, to convey the works employees to and from the trams. When starting and finishing times were during the hours of darkness, Lamplough's "Covered Wagon" as it was called, was illuminated by a couple of candle lamps, and looked for all the world like something from the Middle West, or a flash-back to the Voertrekkers in the Transvaal.

Once or twice, when my bicycle was out of action, I managed to get a lift on this vehicle to Marfleet. One ocasion I particularly remember: driver Lamplough just could not get his horses to start on the homeward run. Coaxing, wearing and whipping were all tried without success, and the prospective passengers gathered round to give what encouragement they could, or take the mickey out of the harrassed driver, now almost at his wit's end. Suddenly, as if stung by the sarcastic remarks of the spectators, the horses leapt into life, and galloped off down the road like potential Derby winners. About half a dozen of the younger element, including myself, managed to leap on board, and the "chariot" swept round the corner on two wheels, leaving the unfortunate ones to face an almost three-mile walk to Marfleet, for the horses could not then be pulled up, and we reached the tram terminus in record time. Meanwhile we lucky ones were nearly in hysterics at the turn of events, and the thought of the angry remnant trudging homeward.

It was in the August of 1918 that the German armies on the Western Front began to crumble. They had taken a hammering on 18th July when Foch made his memorable attack at Villers Cotterets with tank cover, and this advantage was driven home on 8th August when the British took the offensive on the Somme front, with over four hundred tanks. At last, the once derided tank was proving its value, and the German Army had no counter. Locally, and for me at any rate, this offensive recalled the earlier "Tank Week," when cities and towns were exhorted to buy War Loan, and a specimen tank was parked in the City Square, outside the City Hall. The public were invited to contribute to the fund, and there was usually a queue of people waiting to have a peep inside this strange new instrument of war. Hull's total towards the fund was £13 million, well above the national average, the total raised being about £500 million.

Dispirited as their high command was at the thought of the immense American man-power in reserve, the Germans knew that the war was lost, and their main thought was to finish the conflict outside their own territory. A general retreat started, and by early November, disorganised and war-weary, they were ready to accept an armistice based on President Wilson's famous fourteen points.

At home, excitement grew as the longed-for day drew near. On the morning of November 11th I had cycled to Salt End as usual, and had done the normal routine jobs. At 11 a.m., all the hooters on Humberside, which had in the previous few years dolefully boomed out their air-raid warnings, suddenly sprang to life in a joyous burst of sound which rose and fell, and rose

A typical 1917 tank, as seen in "Tank Week," Hull City Square, 1917.

again like a great anthem expressing the pent-up emotions of a tired but eminently courageous people, and at that precious moment, the armistice was being signed in a railway carriage in northern France.

In our works, a tremendous cheer broke out as the sirens sounded, and a spontaneous down tools was the signal for all except key workers and management to make for home and celebrations. Office staff and management shook hands, and as soon as possible a complete shut-down was made. A few of the staff made for Paull to have a celebration at the "Royal Oak," a favourite local hostelry, while I took the earliest opportunity to get on my bicycle and cycle home. After a quick meal with everybody chattering, and Mother rather bewildered at the turn of events, I caught a tram for the city centre. There, cheering crowds packed Queen Victoria Square, and some adventurous elements swarmed up the statue of the old queen, balancing uneasily, and tossing their hats into the crowd below. Presumably she was "not amused" at this indignity to her person, yet perhaps even she sympathised with the tremendous feeling of relief that it was all over!

Down Whitefriargate where I went next, mingling with the happy and jostling crowds, there was a sudden commotion and a tradesman's box tricycle, apparently commandeered from some unsuspecting errand boy, appeared. Pushed by two brawny jack tars, with two more standing on the box trying to execute what looked like a hornpipe or a naval two-step, the crazy vehicle careered along Whitefriargate with the crowd tumbling over themselves to make a narrow passageway. This incident was typical of the wild and joyous abandon of Armistice Day. The war was over, and nothing else mattered.

It was later on that the nation found time to reflect on the awful price paid for victory — a million dead and many more crippled in the British Empire alone. One of the saddest incidents I heard of, was the mother at South Ferriby who having already lost two of her three sons, received a telegram, while the bells were pealing the news of the armistice, telling her that her last and youngest son had been killed in action.

Just about this time, the great influenza epidemic was gaining momentum. Spreading westward across most of the world, the deadly virus claimed more victims in the next few months than even the war itself. I, fortunately as it happened, had had a mild dose of the 'flu in July of that year, and must have gained some immunity, for I escaped the main onslaught. At its height, there were only two of us in the office on duty, while at home my mother, sister and brother were all ill at the same time, and I had to cope as well as I could, tending the needs of the family before setting off for work and after returning home. This "Spanish" 'flu attacked all sections of society, young and old, anaemic or healthy. In the fatal cases, the high temperatures, aching bones and lassitude, were followed by pneumonia, and the victim would be dead within a few days. A prominent local victim, Sir Mark Sykes, the member of Parliament for Hull Central, was attending the Paris Peace Conference when he contracted it and died. Sir Mark, a specialist in Middle East matters, was spoken of as a future Foreign Secretary and a possible Prime Minister. Another local casualty was Councillor W. C. Dawson, the chairman of the Hull Education Committee. William Dawson was a cousin of my late father, and had just been adopted as Liberal candidate for Peterborough at the forthcoming general election. Yet another victim near to us was one of my sister Dorothy's closest friends. Olga was a lively girl of sixteen, blooming with health, yet she died within four days of contracting the deadly disease.

One of the first matters to receive government attention after the armistice was the repatriation of thousands of prisoners of war. Shipping of many nations was brought in to assist in the task of conveying these men home. On the Humber there was great excitement and enthusiasm when, towards the end of November, a Danish liner, the *Frederick VIII*, arrived in the river with several thousand British ex-prisoners from German camps. At the oil terminal we received news that the ship was due to pass Salt End Oil Jetty shortly before mid-day.

All who could be spared walked the length of the jetty to see the big two-funnelled liner approach. Her tiers of decks were crowded with khaki-clad figures — many had even climbed the rigging — and they waved and cheered as they passed upstream to Hull. There, at reception centres, they were entertained and given clothing if needed, before boarding trains for their home areas and a long delayed reunion with their families and friends. In some cases they had been in prisoner-of-war camps for over four years. Perhaps the record locally was the case of Captain Ford and the crew of one of Wilson's ships which happened to be in the port of Hamburg when war broke out on August 4th 1914, and they were interned for the whole of the war.

A month later, I had my fifteenth birthday. In that relatively short period of my life, much had happened. I had been born in Hull not long after the turn of the century, had spent two happy carefree years in sight of the Humber in North Lincolnshire, returned and seen the Edwardian era succeeded by the Georgian. I had had the traumatic experience of losing my father at the age of eight, and encountered the grim days which followed. Happy schooldays had been succeeded all too quickly by full-time employment at the age of thirteen. I had seen how people on the home front had braced themselves and endured the greatest war of all time. There had been fun and foolishness, satisfaction and setbacks, toil and tragedy.

A childhood lived on both sides of a great waterway and a family life forged in love and adversity.